# THE LATEST SEALINGS

## from the

# PALACE AND HOUSES

## at

# KNOSSOS

by

MERVYN R. POPHAM

and

MARGARET A.V. GILL

Seal from the Evans Collection

BRITISH SCHOOL AT ATHENS

STUDIES: I

ISBN 0 904887 24 3

Printed in Great Britain at the Alden Press, Oxford

To

SIR JOHN BOARDMAN

for his constant support
and encouragement

and

in memory of

DR. ANDREAS KORETSOS

a kind friend and caring doctor
to members of the British School
at Knossos

# Contents

# Authors' Acknowledgements

*M.R.P.*

I am grateful to the many people, by no means all named below, who have helped me bring this project to fulfilment. It could not have got off the ground without the ever ready assistance afforded me by the then Director of the Herakleion Museum, Dr. Ch. Kritsas, and his staff, who made the sealings available to me to photograph on several occasions. In addition, when I was preparing the section on the seals, Alexandra Karetsou patiently and helpfully answered my questions about entries in the Catalogue of that museum. Margaret Gill made an immense contribution not only in revising her original article and agreeing to its publication here, but also in courteously replying to all my many queries about various aspects of the material. Similar expert advice and support were given me on various occasions by John Younger, and by Judith Weingarten whose article 'Seal-use and Administration in the South-West Basement Area at Knossos' in *BSA* 89 (1994) 151–6, arrived too late to be taken into account.

My photographs, not always of the best quality, were enlarged to scale with great care by Bob Wilkins of the Institute of Archaeology at Oxford, where I was also provided with much support in other ways. Colin Macdonald kindly rephotographed some sealings which required this, and added others which I had missed. Dimitris Plantzos and Jamie Bell assisted greatly in sorting the photographs and putting them in order, a task for which the Meyerstein Fund made a generous grant.

My researches in the Evans Archive in the Ashmolean Museum were aided at all stages by Ann Brown, one result of which was that all the sketches cut out of his notes by Evans were located and returned to their original positions.

My thanks are due also to John Betts for allowing me to reproduce his published drawings, and to Ingo Pini for similar permission in the case of Her. s. 255 and 1529.

The Trustees of the Estate of Sir Arthur Evans kindly agreed to the reproduction of passages relevant to the sealings from the notebooks of Evans and Mackenzie.

The manuscript was typed in several drafts and in its final state with her customary care by Lynda Smithson at the Institute of Archaeology.


*M.A.V.G.*

I am most grateful to Dr. S. Alexiou, Director of the Herakleion Archaeological Museum, to Dr. N. Platon, the Museum's ex-Director, and to Dr. H.W. Catling, Curator of the Classical Antiquities section, Ashmolean Museum, who have made the sealings accessible for my study. I should like especially to thank John Boardman for his advice while I was writing this article and his helpful criticism of it in its final stages. Amendments to the original text of this article take into account work done in collaboration with Prof. Ingo Pini and Dr. Walter Müller on the projected CMS II,8 *Die Siegelabdrücke von Knossos*.

# Abbreviations

*AE/NB*     Arthur Evans's Excavation Notebooks, year and page references.

*AE/HL*     Arthur Evans's Handlist of Linear B Tablets. Reproduced in *OKT* pages 34–5.

Ash. Mus.   Ashmolean Museum, Oxford.

Betts       The numbers given to sealings in J.H. Betts, 'Some Unpublished Knossos Sealings and Sealstones', *BSA* 62 (1967) 27–45.

*Bossert*   H.T. Bossert, *Altkreta* (Berlin, 3rd ed., 1937).

*BSA*       Annual of the British School at Athens.

CMS         Corpus der minoischen und mykenischen Siegel.

*DM/DB*     Day Books of the Knossos Excavations by Duncan Mackenzie, year, date and occasionally page references.

Gill        'The Knossos Sealings; Some Comments' by M.A.V. Gill in *Kadmos* 5 (1966) 1–16.

Her.        Herakleion Museum, Crete. Her. s. = Catalogue numbers of sealings.

HM          Number given to seals in the Inventory of Herakleion Museum.

*JHS*       *Journal of Hellenic Studies.*

*Kenna*     Catalogue number of Ashmolean seals/sealings as given in V.E.G. Kenna, *Cretan Seals* (Oxford, 1960).

Kenna       used in Section 3 with dates refers to the dating given by V.E.G. Kenna in his article 'Seals and Script III, Cretan Seal Use and the Dating of Linear B Script', *Kadmos* 3 (1964) 29–59.

NM          National Museum, Athens.

*OKT*       L.R. Palmer and J. Boardman, *On the Knossos Tablets* (Oxford, 1963).

Ox.         Catalogue numbers of seals/sealings in the Ashmolean Museum, Oxford. Ox. n. No. = Uncatalogued sealings.

*Philia Epi*  *Philia Epi eis G.E. Mylonan* 1–3, Athens 1986–1989.

*PM*        Arthur Evans, *The Palace of Minos at Knossos* Vols. I–IV, London 1921–1935.

*PreT*      A.J. Evans, 'The Prehistoric Tombs of Knossos', *Archaeologia* LIX (1905) 391–562. Also published as a separate monograph, London 1906.

*PZ*        *Prähistorische Zeitschrift.*

*SM*          A.J. Evans, *Scripta Minoa* Vols. I and II.

*SMEA*        *Studi Micenei ed Egeo-Anatolici.*

Younger       used in Section 3 with dates refers to the dating ascribed by J.G. Younger to stylistic groups, not individual sealings, in his series of articles given in Note 12 of Section 1. The last of these, *Kadmos* 28 (1989) 101–136, is a concordance in which the sealings are listed and reference given to the particular article in which individual ones are considered.

# Section 1

# The background to the sealings

M.R. POPHAM

Evans, to his great delight, found the first clay scalings within the palace at Knossos 18 days after he and Mackenzie began excavations there in 1900.[1] They were subsequently to discover in the fire destruction of the final palace some 800 or more, including fragments, the main concentration being in the E. wing of the building, in the so-called Domestic Quarter. Others occurred outside the palace, in the Arsenal and, more particularly, in the Little Palace. Most were fragmentary, and the small size of many of those now housed in Herakleion Museum attest the care with which they were collected; indeed, after the discovery of inscribed tablets, sieving of the excavated soil where they or sealings were present became the customary practice.[2] So, we may be confident that few, if any, went undetected.

Evans already had a long-standing concern with Cretan seals and had collected a considerable number of them during his tour of the island in 1894.[3] He had noticed that some were engraved with signs which he, correctly, thought were an early form of writing – now known as the hieroglyphic script. His interest was drawn, too, to depictions which he recognized had a religious connotation and provided an insight into religious ritual and symbolism. He was also fully appreciative of their artistic merit. In all of this he was aided by an acute short-sightedness which enabled him to examine them close up without a magnifying glass.[4]

It is not therefore surprising that, though overshadowed by the momentous discovery of inscribed tablets, the sealings claimed particular attention from Evans from the very beginning. In his notebook for 1900 he recorded where in that year some had been found and sketched their motives. His facility for recognizing the design and of drawing its main features has subsequently been invaluable in identifying so many of the sealings and enabling them to be given a provenance. In subsequent years, the overall record of the digging was left almost entirely to Mackenzie, while Evans devoted more attention to details and to the finds which particularly interested him. Among these were the sealings which he listed by deposits, giving a very brief description of their design often accompanied by a sketch, noting at the same time how many examples of a particular version he had recognized.

It is probably at this preliminary stage that he selected for drawing those which interested him most, and marked this on his lists. Curiously, none appears to have been photographed though important sherds were. A few of the sealings from the final destruction were illustrated in the *Annual Reports* which appeared the year after each season's excavation. More were subsequently published in Volumes I–III of the *Palace of Minos* as examples of a particular aspect of Minoan civilization which Evans was discussing. A consolidated account, however, was not given until the final, fourth volume in 1936 in which lists were given of the sealings in the major deposits, illustrated by additional drawings, some not without their problems.[5]

Notes Evans made in preparation for this final account have survived, showing how he went through earlier notebooks to bring the material together, repeating his former descriptions and copying the sketches which he had made at certain points in the course of the excavations. There is little indication that he re-examined the sealings themselves, which by then were mostly in Herakleion Museum, and he appears to have relied almost exclusively on his earlier records.[6]

The resultant publication was far from complete. In all he illustrated with drawings some 70 of the latest sealings, well under a third of those whose find places he had recorded. All sealings are not, however, unique impressions; multiple examples from the same signet are not infrequent, though only in a very few instances do they reach as many as twenty duplicates. Even so, the surviving sealings from Knossos provide evidence for the use of well over 250 seals and rings by administrative officials, to which may be added considerably more, if others from the Little Palace recorded by Evans, but now lost, are taken into account.

The extent to which his presentation of this evidence had been selective did not become really apparent until the dispute arose over the date of the final destruction, which focused interest on the original records of the excavation and the surviving material. In this dispute, between the 1400 date of Evans (LM II), supported by Boardman, and one at around 1200 (LM IIIB) or even later proposed by Palmer, the sealings, or rather the signets with which they had been impressed, had an important chronological contribution to make. Not only were sealings often indissolubly linked in context with the tablets but some had themselves been inscribed over the impression or on the back of the nodule with Linear B signs. Not surprisingly, therefore, the book, *On the Knossos Tablets* by L. Palmer and J. Boardman (1963), in which the contesting views were published and the evidence set out to support them, included an appendix on the sealings and their dating by V. Kenna who, for this purpose, had studied all the examples, published and unpublished, which had been catalogued up to that date, 1963, in Herakleion Museum. His conclusion was that Evans's dating was basically correct and that none of the sealings 'carried motifs or patterns associated with LM IIIB use'.[7]

Reasonably, his discussion centred on the thirteen sealings, he had noticed, which were countersigned or endorsed with Linear B signs. These, or rather the signets which had impressed them, were dated on stylistic grounds.[8] A wider perspective was given in his subsequent study in which some of the sealings were held to be very closely related stylistically with seals from burials in the Kalyvia cemetery at Phaestos, dated to early LM IIIA, not long after Evans's date of around 1400 B.C.[9]

Palmer, in his section of *OKT* part III (p. 197), concentrated on questioning the validity of dating seals stylistically. However, he made a useful addition to the published information by reproducing various pages of Evans's notebooks which contained twelve sketches of sealings, as well as one list Evans made of those found in the Little Palace.[10]

Earlier, Kenna in *Cretan Seals* (1960) had included photographs of nine sealings in the Ashmolean Museum ascribable to the final destruction, of which only one had not previously been illustrated by drawings.[11]

These various studies had added little apart from reproducing some of Evans's original sketches, to the evidence given in *PM*, leaving the bulk of the sealings still unpublished. Clearly there was a need for a full publication of the sealings, or at least of those from known contexts. It was the latter, more circumscribed, task which was undertaken by Margaret Gill, who after a meticulous investigation into all the early records and having studied all the then known sealings, published an article in *BSA* 60 (1965) 58–98. Apart from one important deposit, she was able to identify most of the actual sealings which Evans had sketched as well as a few others where his descriptions were sufficiently precise. The exception was those found in the Little Palace the great majority of which had been lost. That article remains fundamental to any account of the sealings, and I am grateful to her for agreeing that its text be reproduced here insofar as it relates to the deposits belonging to the final destruction. It has been brought up-to-date mainly to take account of subsequent identifications made possible by the discovery of previously unknown sealings in Herakleion Museum.

The opportunity has been taken at the same time to make certain changes and additions for ease of use and to provide additional information.

The enlargements of Evans's sketches of individual sealings, given in that article, have been replaced by reproductions at near life size of the pages and passages of Evans's notebooks in which those drawings occur (PLATES 33–47). Onto these extracts have been superimposed the numbers allocated by Gill to each sealing.

Her references to where final drawings were published have been substituted by reference to Plates in this volume where, for ease of reference, those drawings, scattered through various volumes of *PM*, have been collected together and reproduced at a near uniform scale. The source of these can now be found in the captions to those Plates. Drawings published since these, mainly by John Betts, have been included and plate references to these added to her lists.

For those interested in the circumstances in which the sealings were found, she has added references to pages in *OKT* where passages from the notebooks are quoted which provide this information.

The present publication would have been largely unnecessary had she been permitted to reproduce the photographs she had taken of the sealings. However, at the time, the material had been reserved by the then Ephor who was collaborating with Professor Matz in preparations for their publication in a volume of the CMS, a project which later ran into difficulties and was not completed. Consequently, she was able to reproduce only Evans's sketches and descriptions to support her identifications. This left any true appreciation of the nature, quality and style of the originals impossible except where drawings had been published by Evans.

Since her study, no comprehensive survey of the sealings has appeared, though individual impressions have been discussed. This is, no doubt, in part because they have not been fully published. However, the illustrated examples have been included in a series of articles by John Younger, whose main purpose has been to ascribe seals and engraved rings to broad stylistic groups, arranged in chronological order with suggested ranges of dates.[12]

The consequences of these and other studies to the dating of the latest Knossos sealings will be further considered in Section 4. At this stage, it may be remarked that they appear to be consistent with the dating given by Evans, modified slightly by the somewhat later chronology, around 1375 BC, called LM IIIA 1, now generally adopted for the final destruction. No signet, responsible for any of the sealings is, as yet, ascribed to the thirteenth century.

Apart from sealings, Evans found a number of actual seals (remarkably few considering the care taken in sieving the excavated soil), none of which was used to impress any extant sealing.[13] It seemed opportune to review this evidence as well, in Section 5, since it has so far received little attention and there are errors which need correction. The excavation notebooks provide evidence about where some of them were found, but they appear never to have been listed and mostly to have escaped Evans's attention. Indeed those found in the excavations of 1902, according to the inventory of Herakleion Museum, received no mention in either the *Annual Reports* or *PM*. The few later such finds, with the exception of one seal from the Little Palace, were similarly overlooked. Related evidence for the existence of a sealmaker's workshop in the S.W. region of the Palace was, however, considered and presented by Evans; this has subsequently been reviewed, after a study of the material, by J. Younger.[14]

The full publication of the sealings in CMS is, it is understood, now well advanced and it is to that work which serious students of them will ultimately turn for details of size, shape, condition and for accurate drawings. Such information is not given here, where the main purpose is to complement Gill's article with photographs, and to present the evidence on which her identifications were based. Additionally, some 110 sealings have been included which were not recorded by Evans and which, consequently, have no context though their association with the final destruction seems likely and, indeed, probable. They have been selected largely on account of their legibility or the interest of their subject matter.

For a full coverage of these too, readers will have to await the projected volume of the CMS in which they will be published. Though, therefore, to some extent only partial, it is hoped that this publication will stimulate a wider discussion of the various aspects of the sealings than has hitherto been possible.

Certain aspects of them and their use have concerned the author in the preparation of this publication. No expert himself in this field, he nevertheless hopes that some of the observations and ideas included in Section 4 might be thought worth pursuing further by those who are.

## NOTES

1. As Evans recorded in his notebook for April 10th 1900, reproduced at PLATE 36.

2. Mentioned on several occasions, and particularly stressed by Evans in *BSA* 6 (1899–1900) 69. Clearly, sealings were missed in the digging and only recovered afterwards in sieving the excavated soil. Mackenzie (14/3/1901) records 'As many as 20 fragments were got by this means' in the area which became known as the Room of the Seal Impressions. Since he had previously, on 9/3/1901, recorded the finding by similar means of Q 13, recognizable from his detailed description, this would imply that few, if any, of the 28 sealings listed by Evans were found in the actual digging.

3. *JHS* 21 (1901) 99–204.

4. We are informed of Evans's shortsightedness by Joan Evans in her biography *Time and Chance*. On his early interest in religious symbolism, see for instance his article 'Mycenaean Tree and Pillar-Cult', *JHS* 21 (1901) 170f.

5. *PM* IV.591–618. Evans may have possessed additional notes to those which have survived, or been located, which provided the evidence for his inclusion of some more sealings than are recorded in his extant notes in the lists he gave in *PM* IV. They are, however, suspect at times, especially his supplementary list for the Domestic Quarter (lists C and D), which contain some clear errors of provenance. It may be that at this late stage he discovered drawings of sealings without a record of their find spots, and assumed, somewhat arbitrarily, that they had come from the Domestic Quarter where most of the sealings had been found.

6. Had he re-examined the sealings in any detail, he would surely have selected out for drawing such sealings as Her. s. 147 as another example of the use of the impaled triangle, Her. s. 370 (with 381) as an outstanding depiction of a marine scene with dolphins, and Her. s. 378 for its religious importance, with its shrine, adorant and figure-of-eight shield (PLATES 19–20).

7. *OKT* 98.

8. His account was later expanded by M. Gill in *Kadmos* 5 (1966) 1–16, who gave abbreviated sketches of the designs on the sealings and added inscribed nodules without impressions, but was not concerned with dating.

9. *Kadmos* 3 (1964) 29–57, where he is relying on Furumark's dating in *Chronology* 104–5 who had classified the latest destruction pottery as LM IIIA 1.

10. His illustrations, Plates III, V-VII, IX-X, XXIII and XXVIII.

11. *Cretan Seals* p. 147, 40S to 52S (omitting 44S), and corresponding Plates there.

12. *Kadmos* 21 (1982) 104–21 (with J. Betts), *Kadmos* 22 (1983) 109–36, *Kadmos* 23 (1984) 38–64, *Kadmos* 24 (1985) 34–78, *Kadmos* 25 (1986) 119–40, *Kadmos* 26 (1987) 44–73 and *Kadmos* 28 (1989) 101–36. Discussed in Section 3.

13. Contrast the few Evans found with the 26 seals from the Unexplored Mansion excavation, 15 from various LM levels, and the remainder from post-Minoan contexts. Mr. Sinclair Hood has kindly informed me that in his excavations in the Royal Road (North) some 34 seals were recovered, mostly in Minoan levels. Evans's sieving should have discovered any which had been missed in the digging. This could imply that few seals were in use inside the Palace building.

14. *BSA* 74 (1979) 258–68. As pointed out to me by Sinclair Hood, there is no record of the finding of the engraved steatite core or of the roughed-out sealstones in any of the notebooks. They are first mentioned and illustrated in *PM* IV.594–5 in Evans's discussion of the 'Lapidary's Workshop'.

# Section 2

# The Knossos sealings: provenance and identification

MARGARET A.V. GILL

*REVISED TEXT OF* BSA *60 (1965) 58–98*

*in so far as it relates to sealings associated with the final destruction of the Palace and houses, with corrections and additions by the author. New material has been incorporated only if it correlates with sketches or descriptions in the excavation notebooks.*

*The arbitrary sequence of numbers previously allocated to uncatalogued sealings has been replaced by those now entered in Herakleion Museum Inventory. Moreover, some renumbering of sealings has been made since the article was written: in these cases, the present museum numbers have been substituted. A table correlating the old with the new numbers is given in Concordance B.*

*Since all drawings published by Evans are reproduced in this volume, reference is given to the PLATE on which they appear, while their place of publication, previously included in the text, has been transferred to the captions of those illustrations.*

*In the following discussion single capitals plus numerals refer to sealings listed in the tables at the end of each geographical section.*

Basic to a study of the Knossos sealings from the excavations of Sir Arthur Evans at the beginning of the century are questions of provenance and identification. Seal-impressed nodules were excavated from various parts of the Main Palace and its dependencies, both as isolated finds and as hoards. What sealings were found in which places? And how many can be identified with actual examples in Herakleion and Oxford? Those are the two questions to be considered in this section.

The documents available for this research vary in reliability. Among published accounts, reports in *BSA* have the virtue of being written in the same year as the excavation, though even they are subject to occasional errors arising out of misread notes. *SM* I, compiled a few years later, contains a more mature assessment of the material but is mainly limited to the Hieroglyphic Deposit. More detailed information is to be found in *PM* I–IV; but because of the time that elapsed between the important excavation seasons at the beginning of the century and the publication of this work, the advantage of Evans's greater experience of Minoan archaeology is outweighed by a greater tendency for mistakes to enter unnoticed. Misreading of his own notes and the study of drawings prepared for publication rather than the original material produced the majority of these. The latter practice explains how various seal-stones such as Ox. 1941. 246 (C55) and Her. 845 (E13) not only came to be described as sealings but were also ascribed to specific deposits.

Useful in checking the published accounts but even more important in supplying additional information are the Excavation Notebooks that were never intended for publication. For details about the general extent and limitations of these and relevant quotations from them see *OKT*. So far as a study of the sealings is concerned *DM/DB* (Duncan Mackenzie's Day Books) give the date and circumstances of excavation, whether sealings were found in the course of digging or whether they were salvaged from the sieves. In neither case is it always clear to what context the sealings belong. In the first season Mackenzie appears to have noted the continuation of work in each area even when there was nothing of significance to report (though the strange irregularity of dates on which certain quarters were dug, leaves scope for doubt). In later seasons it is patent that in several instances clearing had taken place and finds been made prior to any entry in the Notebook, the first record being a statement of the stage reached by the *beginning* of that day's excavation. Such omissions make correlation with *AE/NB* (Arthur Evans's Notebooks) more difficult, as for example in confirming the location of R100–1 or the Little Palace sealings. But it is only in conjunction with *AE/NB* that *DM/DB* can be used, as the latter rarely contain descriptions of sealings and have no sketches of them to facilitate identification.

*AE/NB* usually gives the name of the room and occasionally a more detailed account of the circumstances under which the finds were made, but its main value lies in the numerous descriptions and/or sketches. Particular problems in interpreting the information I shall discuss below at the beginning of each section. A general difficulty is how to deal with apparent discrepancies between the published versions and the Notebook evidence; the former are not necessarily always wrong. It must be remembered that Evans did not record every sealing and although there are over a thousand nodules in Herakleion and Oxford, many are still missing, especially those from the Little Palace. Thus it is always possible when the two accounts differ in their location of a particular impression, that more than one copy may have been found, the published account being based on memory or other lists and notes since mislaid.

Often, however, the conflicting versions are the result of mistakes produced by hasty study of the Notebooks in compiling catalogues or ascertaining provenance, and of a failure to notice that all the sealings on a particular page are not from a single source (e.g. K1–4). At some date Evans cut various of the drawings from their contexts, which may account for other muddles in *PM*. Fortunately all of the cuttings have been preserved and have now been restored to their original positions.

More of a problem is the terminology applied to the areas being excavated, names that were later abandoned. Although it did not prevent him from falling into the trap of mistaking the contents of Magazine 8 for those of Magazine 5 (G6), Evans was himself aware of the danger of this type of confusion and made additional comments or alterations in the Notebooks giving the later nomenclature, as for example when he clarified Gallery H1 (*sic*, H4, cf. Plan of the Palace, *BSA* 7 (1900–1), for this grid-reference) as the Gallery of the Jewel Fresco or Magazine of the Vase Tablets. Sometimes the clarification itself is misleading or even inexact, the result of later interpretation of the material (cf. Section Q).

*AE/NB* is the main source for learning what seals came from each deposit and for identifying the actual examples in the museums. In a few instances another body of material has proved useful, drawings prepared for publication but never reproduced. The type of penwork used to depict Her. s. 386, 397, 405 (L24, Lb, L8–12) shows that they were drawn on the same occasion as Her. s. 396 (L48) and others from the Temple Repository. When Evans was making the entries relating to the Little Palace in *AE/NB* 1905, he had already decided which sealings to have specially drawn; these he marked with an asterisk, but did not bother to sketch them. Correlation of these descriptions and the drawings make several identifications possible, and their association with other sealings (drawn and undrawn) in the same range of Herakleion catalogue numbers suggests that some of the latter may also have come from the Little Palace.

The Museum Acquisition Catalogues are on the whole uninformative. As the Oxford sealings were not acquired by the Ashmolean until 1938 the only details of provenance are those derived from *PM*, other than the simple attribution to Knossos of a few unpublished nodules. More can be deduced from the Herakleion Catalogue. The first and main batch of Knossos sealings to enter this museum were those belonging to the 1900–1904 seasons (Her. s. 106–413). No specific locations are given but sometimes among the identifiable impressions a pattern is observable; sealings within a certain range of numbers appear to belong to the same deposit (e.g. Her. s. 170–200 from the Hieroglyphic Deposit; 333–52, 383–97 from the Temple Repository). This is what one would expect of finds delivered to the museum in the same boxes and envelopes in which they had been stored during work on the site. However, too much weight should not be given to this as a method of placing otherwise unidentified sealings, for elsewhere the catalogue entries are patently haphazard. A second group of sealings mainly from the Little Palace reached the museum in 1908 (Her. s. 415–26). Her. s. 650–60 had probably become mislaid after being drawn for Evans, and together with 661–71 (found in 1922 under circumstances described in *JHS* 45 (1925) 17, *PM* IV.451–2) were later rediscovered in a museum drawer and catalogued in 1940. Among these Her. s. 661–5, 667, 671 are recorded as coming from the Treasury of the Domestic Quarters. In more recent years other sealings from Knossos have either turned up in the museum itself or in the pottery stores of the Palace. In the 1960s some hundred such were arranged uncatalogued in wooden trays with the compartments labelled in Greek. As the sealings themselves were not marked, accidental shuffling inevitably took place, giving rise to considerable confusion. In *BSA* 60 (1965) I quoted the two series of numbering as they were in 1960 and 1963; other scholars on different occasions apparently found them otherwise arranged. Another 81 sealings, published by J.H. Betts in *BSA* 62 (1967) 27–45, were found by M.R. Popham in two boxes in the Stratigraphical Museum. Whether they came from the same quarters of the Palace as the pottery associated with them in the storerooms is a matter for conjecture; comparison with other sealings casts doubt on the assumption that they were originally associated. Since then further groups of sealings have come to light amongst Evans's excavation material, and miscellaneous sealings have been excavated from trial trenches within the Main Palace and its environs. As nearly all the Knossos sealings currently located in Herakleion Museum are now catalogued, I include in Concordance B a correlation between the numbering I used in *BSA* 60 (1965) and the new Museum inventory numbers.

Evidence from the actual sealings for attributing them to particular deposits is not limited solely to the identification of the motifs. Usually a sufficient number of sealings can be identified beyond doubt from external evidence to determine the general character of each deposit, the glyptic style, colour range of the clay, and the usage of the nodules. Applied to doubtful identifications these considerations help to confirm or eliminate, also to distinguish between several examples of the same motif when they occur in different deposits and to suggest other examples that should possibly be included in a deposit. Of the three nodules impressed with the same kneeling bull design, for instance, only Her. s. 295 and Her. s. 329 can be identified with *AE/NB* sketches (K6, R46); the third, Her. s. 1208 (PLATE 17), in all probability belongs to the same deposit as one of these. Sealings from the Room of the Jewel Fresco (K1–10) have been baked to a uniform deep red, so the blackened condition of Her. s. 1208 is more in keeping with the deposit in the Lower East-West Corridor (R38–52) where local variation in the intensity of the conflagration, degree of oxidation, etc., has produced a wider colour range, from bright orange to dark brown and black. The style of the curvilinear designs on Her. s. 390/1–2 resembles that of Her. s. 374 (L1–6), and the pale colour, shape and narrow perforation of both nodules correspond with several other sealings typical of the Temple Repository, leaving little doubt that they belong to the same deposit. Similarly Her. s. 1260 finds parallels in the reddened clay and disk shapes impressed round the edges, suggesting common derivation with Her. s. 343–6 from the Temple Repository.

With such a complex body of material it has been a problem deciding the most lucid method of presentation. For simplicity I have divided it into sections according to geographical distribution. References are given to the relevant entries in the Notebooks and Evans's publications, and to quotations from the Notebooks in *OKT* at the beginning of each section. These are followed by comments on details of location provided by the Notebooks that have not already appeared in publication, discussion of problems arising from them, of questions of identification and conflicting accounts. More important are the tables that follow, in which evidence from *AE/NB* is correlated with the material in Herakleion and Oxford. This seems to be the most intelligible way of arrangement though it has one unavoidable drawback: concentrating the information into tabulated form means that minor problems and petty corrections receive undue emphasis from the necessity to include them in the preliminary discussion. Contradictions and errors inevitably creep into any study and it is not surprising to discover them in work as extensive as Evans's. They need pointing out and explaining but such comments should not be allowed to detract from the importance of Evans's basic work and the conclusions that may be drawn from it.

## EXPLANATION OF TABLES AT THE END OF EACH SECTION

Col. 1    My reference. The lettering begins at F to avoid confusion with Evans's catalogues (cf. below, Col. 7) and letters I and P have not been used. The numbering is not indicative of the actual number of sealings found in each deposit but the number described and/ or sketched in *AE/NB* (or rarely in *DM/DB*).

Col. 2    An asterisk (*) indicates the existence of a sketch of the sealing by Evans.

Col. 3    An asterisk (*) indicates that the sealing was described by Evans (or rarely by Mackenzie) whether or not it was also sketched.

Col. 4    An asterisk (*) indicates that Evans had the sealing drawn for publication, though some were not used. For details see captions to plates.

Col. 5    Herakleion or Oxford sealing identified with sketch or description; several numbers are given if the sketch is a composite design.

Col. 6    Catalogue numbers of other sealings bearing the same motif, belonging or probably belonging to the same deposit.

Col. 7    Cross-reference to Evans's catalogues:

> A  S.W. Basements (Q)
> B  Central Shrine (M)
> C  Archives
> D  East Hall Borders
> E  Little Palace (U)
> } (R) } *PM* IV.601–6

Col. 8    (*a*) Description quoted from *AE/NB* when there is no sketch.
          (*b*) Comments on any difference between *AE/NB* figure and actual sealing.
          (*c*) Reference to plates in this volume or other published illustrations.
          (*d*) Cross-reference to examples of the same motif on sealings in other deposits. On the first occasion all other examples are noted; subsequently reference is only made to the first.

Additional tables (A–E in list above) occur at the ends of Sections M, Q, R and U:

Col. i.    Evans's reference (*PM* IV.601–6).
Col. ii.   Cross-reference to my numbering.
Col. iii.  Herakleion or Oxford Catalogue number.
Col. iv.   Plate references and other comments.

Published sealings that occur neither in *AE/NB* nor in Evans's lists A–E I have noted at the end of the appropriate sections, distinguishing them with alphabetic instead of numerical references.

## F.  SOUTH-WEST CORNER (Plan at PLATE 1,1–2)

> *AE/NB* 1900.24, 27.
> *OKT* 69, pl. III.

F1 was found while earth round the Cupbearer Fresco was being cleared (PLATE 1,2) and F2 came to light 'near the S.W. door', i.e. south of the doorway west of the Corridor of the Cupbearer Fresco (PLATE 1,1).

| Ref. no. | Sketch | Description | Drawing | Sealing | Other examples | AE Cat. | Comments and plate reference |
|----------|--------|-------------|---------|---------|----------------|---------|------------------------------|
| F1 | * | * | | Her. s. 123 | | | PLATES 2 and 33. |
| F2 | * | * | | Her. s. 258/2 | | | 'hind quarters of a lion' (*sic*, standing bitch). cf. K4. PLATES 2 and 33. |

## G.  WEST MAGAZINES

*Section of wall near Magazine 3* (Plan at PLATE 1,3)

> *AE/NB* 1905.12 *bis*.
> *BSA* 11 (1904–5) 21.
> *OKT* 101.

| Ref. no. | Sketch | Description | Drawing | Sealing | Other examples | AE Cat. | Comments and plate reference |
|---|---|---|---|---|---|---|---|
| G1 | * | | | | | | 'Demon'. |

*Magazine 4* (Gallery 5) (Plan at PLATE 1,4)

*AE/NB* 1900.60, 70; *DM/DB* 1900, May 2.
*SM* I.159, P51.
*OKT* 34, 92.

G3 (Her. s. 240) is part of a much larger circular design depicting two symmetrically arranged bulls walking with heads down and feet towards the centre, so that the head of each almost touches the hindleg of the other. There can be no doubt that Her. s. 1023 is a larger fragment of the same design but derived from the opposite half of the composition since it has a convex outline to the bull's ear where that of Her. s. 240 is concave (cf. PLATE 32(a)). However, while the other sealings from Magazine 4 are red and (apart from G2 which is an unperforated knob) bear the impression of a coarse type of string, Her. s. 1023 is black and perforated by a fine thread. So similar is its shape and condition to G6 that, serving the same purpose, they may have come from the same magazine. G4(?) may be a qualification of G3 rather than the description of a separate sealing. In *SM* I.159 G2 has been included with sealings from the Hieroglyphic Deposit.

| Ref. no. | Sketch | Description | Drawing | Sealing | Other examples | AE Cat. | Comments and plate reference |
|---|---|---|---|---|---|---|---|
| G2 | * | * | * | Her. s. 107 | | | *SM* I, 159, P51, pls. III, IVA. |
| G3 | * | * | | Her. s. 240 | Her. s. 1023 | | PLATES 2, 17, 27 and 33. |
| | | | | | Her. s. 1542 | | |
| G4(?) | | * | | | | | 'perhaps(?) part of larger galloping bull'. PLATE 33. |
| G5 | * | * | | Her. s. 239 | Her. s. 241 | | PLATES 2 and 33. cf. G6. |

*Magazine 8* (Gallery 9, Gallery of Pithoi (Plan at PLATE 1,5)

*AE/NB* 1900.50 *bis*; *DM/DB* 1900, April 26.
*SM* I.42; *PM* III.230; IV.617–18, 620.
*OKT* 95.

By tracing the course of excavation in the W. Magazines it is clear that the term 'Gallery of Pithoi' applied first to Magazine 8, and that it was here on April 26 that G6 was unearthed. Evans's consistent attribution of the sealing to Magazine 5 in publication, despite the fact that digging did not begin there until May 1st, may be because in his mind this magazine had become the 'Gallery of the Pithoi' *par excellence*; possibly he recognized that two fragments from Magazine 4 (G5) were impressions of the same seal.

| Ref. no. | Sketch | Description | Drawing | Sealing | Other examples | AE Cat. | Comments and plate reference |
|---|---|---|---|---|---|---|---|
| G6 | * | * | * | Ox. 1938. 1080 | | | PLATES 2, 27 and 33. Kenna 52S. cf. G5. |

*Magazine 9* (Plan at PLATE 1,6)

*AE/NB* 1901.1 *bis*.

By a slip of the pen G7 was first ascribed to Magazine 10, but was immediately corrected to Magazine 9.

| Ref. no. | Sketch | Description | Drawing | Sealing | Other examples | AE Cat. | Comments and plate reference |
|---|---|---|---|---|---|---|---|
| G7 | * | * | | Her. s. 137 | | | PLATES 2 and 33. |

*Magazine 10* (Plan at PLATE 1,7)

*AE/NB* 1901.6; *DM/DB* 1901, March 11.
*BSA* 7 (1900–1) 40; *PM* IV.626.
*OKT* 97.

There appear to be three conflicting accounts of the position of G8 in this magazine: *DM/DB* 'a little above the floor-level', *BSA* 'over the wall of the Tenth Magazine', and *PM* IV 'in the upper filling'. These apparent contradictions may only be the result of a certain ambiguity in the wording; both published versions can be reconciled with *DM/DB*. In *BSA* reference to

G8 comes in a section on the Eleventh Magazine. Evans may have meant that the sealing was found over the wall from Magazine 11, in Magazine 10. His intention in *PM* IV was perhaps to distinguish the contents of the magazine found above floor level from those in the floor cists.

| Ref. no. | Sketch | Description | Drawing | Sealing | Other examples | AE Cat. | Comments and plate reference |
|----------|--------|-------------|---------|---------|----------------|---------|------------------------------|
| G8 | * | * | * | Her. s. 136 | | | *AE/NB* fig. and his illustration interpret the second animal body as corn. PLATES 2, 27 and 33. |

*Magazine 11* (Plan at PLATE 1,8)

> *AE/NB* 1901.6 *bis*, 7; *DM/DB* 1901, March 15, April 1.
> *BSA* 7 (1900–1) 40; *PM* IV.534.
> *OKT* 97, pl. X.

*DM/DB* 1901, March 15 mentions 'a very large gem-impression (about ½)' found in sieving soil from this magazine, and the excavation of a 'clay impression in fragments, of a large seal'. This latter corresponds to G10; the former may therefore be either Her. s. 376/1 or 376/2, both of which show about half of the same design. The attribution of G11 to the Archives Deposit (*PM* IV.534) is probably an error that came about through the misplacement of the sketch cut from *AE/NB*. *PM* IV.535, fig. 486 ascribed to the Little Palace, is, apart from confusion in the drawing of the animals' heads, so close in detail to Her. s. 209 (G10) as to suggest identity.

| Ref. no. | Sketch | Description | Drawing | Sealing | Other examples | AE Cat. | Comments and plate reference |
|----------|--------|-------------|---------|---------|----------------|---------|------------------------------|
| G9 | | * | | Her. s. 376/1 | Her. s. 376/2 | | PLATES 2 and 25. cf. G10. |
| G10 | * | * | * | Her. s. 209 | | | PLATES 2, 25, 27 and 34. cf. G9. |
| G11 | * | * | * | Her. s. 113 | | | PLATES 2, 27 and 34. |
| G12 | * | * | | Her. s. 165 | | | PLATES 3 and 34. |

*Magazines 12 and 13* (here omitted as being an earlier deposit)

*Magazine 15* (Plan at PLATE 1,9)

> *AE/NB* 1901.6 *bis*, 9; *DM/DB* 1901, March 18.
> *BSA* 7 (1900–1) 43; *PM* IV.706 n.3.
> *OKT* 99, pl. X.

| Ref. no. | Sketch | Description | Drawing | Sealing | Other examples | AE Cat. | Comments and plate reference |
|----------|--------|-------------|---------|---------|----------------|---------|------------------------------|
| G13 | * | * | | Her. s. 284 | | | *AE/NB* fig. omits the legs of the hinder animal. PLATES 3 and 34. |
| G14 | * | * | | Her. s. 285 | | | 'another ?lions' gate scheme'. *AE/NB* fig. interprets the legs of the second animal as a pedestal. PLATES 3 and 34. |
| G15 | * | * | * | Ox. 1938. 861 | | | PLATES 3, 27 and 34. Kenna 50S. |
| G16 | | * | | | | | 'another with part of a similar design', i.e. like G15. PLATE 34. |

*Magazine 18* (Plan at PLATE 1,10)

> *AE/NB* 1901.10 *bis*; *DM/DB* 1901, March 16.
> *OKT* pl. IXa.

| Ref. no. | Sketch | Description | Drawing | Sealing | Other examples | AE Cat. | Comments and plate reference |
|----------|--------|-------------|---------|---------|----------------|---------|------------------------------|
| G17 | * | | | Her. s. 193 | | | Inscribed nodule without impression. *DM/DB* notes 'two fragments of (the same) inscription' found the previous day. |

## H.  HIEROGLYPHIC DEPOSIT (here omitted as being an earlier deposit)

## J.  NORTHERN QUARTER

*North of the Room of the Stirrup Jars* (Plan at PLATE 1,11)

> *DM/DB* 1901, April 6.
> *OKT* 123.

Mackenzie records occasional fragments of tablets and sealings as having turned up in the course of several days' excavation south of the North Door Jambs (i.e. North Portico). In a more specific reference to the previous day's work, he mentions inscriptions found at the foot of the north face of the north wall of the Room of the Stirrup Jars under the floor, and follows immediately with a description of the 'clay seal with a stag r. (?) looking back ... countersigned across the impression ... some signs on the back', in all probability from the same place. There can be little doubt as to its identification with Her. s. 129, of which a drawing was made but never published; further sealings of the same type in Oxford may have come from the same area.

| Ref. no. | Sketch | Description | Drawing | Sealing | Other examples | AE Cat. | Comments and plate reference |
|---|---|---|---|---|---|---|---|
| J1 | * | | * | Her. s. 129 | Ox. 1938. 1016 Ox. 1938. 1152 Her. s. 1628 | | PLATE 3. Kenna 45S. *BSA* 60 (1965) pl. 5. |

*Northern Entrance Passage* (Plan at PLATE 1,12–13)

*AE/NB* 1900.69, 72; *DM/DB* 1900, May 11.
*BSA* 6 (1899–1900) 44, 50; *PM* II.243, IV.567, 827.
*OKT* 34, 121–2, pls. XV, XVIa.

*AE/NB* 1900.69 locates J2 with a deposit of tablets *in* the Room of the Spiral Cornice (cf. *BSA* 6 (1899–1900) 44), while on a sketch-plan (*AE/NB* 1900.67) its position is plotted in the passageway to the east, corresponding to *DM/DB* 'The Area to the S. of room 6' (Area of the Bull Relief) 'and E. of the miniature fresco room' (Room of the Spiral Cornice) (PLATE 1,13). J3–5 were excavated further north in the Entrance Passage (PLATE 1,12).

| Ref. no. | Sketch | Description | Drawing | Sealing | Other examples | AE Cat. | Comments and plate reference |
|---|---|---|---|---|---|---|---|
| J2 | * | * | * | Her. s. 109 | NM 5404α | | PLATES 3, 27, 32 and 34. |
| J3 | * | * | * | Her. s. 146 | | | PLATES 3, 27 and 34. |
| J4 | * | | | Her. s. 125 | | | Inscribed nodule without impression. |
| J5 | | * | | | | | 'hind part of bull'. |

## K. AREA OF THE JEWEL FRESCO

*AE/NB* 1901.17, 26, 28 *bis*, 29; *DM/DB* 1901, April 4, 8, 9.
*BSA* 7 (1900–1) 50; *PM* I.695, 716–17, II.764, III.313, IV.544, 563, 601.
*OKT* 106–7, 111–12.

Deposits of sealings were found in two contiguous magazines between the Long Corridor and the Stepped Portico. K1–4 from the Magazine of the Vase Tablets (Gallery of the Jewel Fresco) were accidentally located in Gallery H1 (middle of the West Court, cf. Plan of the Palace, *BSA* 7 (1900–1) for these grid-references) instead of H4 (*AE/NB* 1901.17), and an error arising from the arrangement of the Notebook entries caused them to be published as coming from the Room of the Seal Impressions. Another concentration of sealings occurred by the north wall of the adjacent magazine (Room of the Warrior Seal) as well as three stray fragments in its south-west corner. K2 and K11 appear to be the only copies of that design; its inclusion among those from the Archives Deposit (C2) may have arisen from mistaken identification with the 'ritual scene' when another type (R1) was intended. The original inscription beside the sketch of K4 read '& part of do. Another do. in room E', an additional comment '3 found' probably including K12 in its total. As Her. s. 299 is without doubt the same fragment as K7, Her. s. 258, Ox. 1938. 1014a and c may be those referred to as K4 and K12, for not only is the clay fired to the same red as all the other sealings from the Room of the Jewel Fresco but like Her. s. 299 the back of each bears the impression of a thick cord. This also occurs on a smaller fragment Ox. n. No.7, which was probably never included in any reckoning as only the dog's tail is preserved.

*Room of the Jewel Fresco* (Plan at PLATE 1,17)

| Ref. no. | Sketch | Description | Drawing | Sealing | Other examples | AE Cat. | Comments and plate reference |
|---|---|---|---|---|---|---|---|
| K1 | * | * | * | Ox. 1938. 981 | | | PLATES 3, 27 and 35. Kenna 6S. |
| K2 | * | * | * | Her. s. 114 | Her. s. 115 Her. s. 168/1 or 2 | | '2 examples & parts of third'. *AE/NB* fig. omits ground line. PLATES 3, 4, 27 and 35. cf. K11, (C2). |

| Ref. no. | Sketch | Description | Drawing | Sealing | Other examples | AE Cat. | Comments and plate reference |
|---|---|---|---|---|---|---|---|
| K3 | * | * | | Her. s. 164 | | | 'uncertain (? fisherman)', PLATES 4 and 35. |
| K4 | * | | * | Ox. 1938. 1014 a, c | Ox. n. No.7 | | '3', PLATES 4, 27 and 35, cf. F2, K7, K12, Q21, R53. |
| K5 | * | * | | Her. s. 297 | | | PLATES 4 and 35. |
| K6 | * | * | | Her. s. 295 | | | PLATES 4 and 35, cf. R46. |
| K7 | * | * | | Her. s. 299 | | | PLATES 4 and 35, cf. K4. |
| K8 | * | * | | Her. s. 167 | | | PLATES 4 and 35. |
| K9 | * | * | | Her. s. 298 | | | PLATES 4 and 35. |
| K10 | * | * | | Her. s. 296 | | | PLATES 4 and 35. |
| Ka | | | | | | | *PM* IV.544, 'a wounded lion among rocks'. |

*Room of the Warrior Seal* (Plan at PLATE 1,18)

| Ref. no. | Sketch | Description | Drawing | Sealing | Other examples | AE Cat. | Comments and plate reference |
|---|---|---|---|---|---|---|---|
| K11 | | * | | Her. s. 168/1 or 2 | | | *DM/DB* 1901, April 9 'part of a clay seal with ritualistic scenes', cf. K2. |
| K12 | | | | Her. s. 258/1 | | | cf. K4, 'another do. in room E.'. PLATES 4, 27 and 35. |
| K13 | * | * | | Her. s. 1219 | | | PLATES 4 and 35. |
| K14 | * | | | | | | PLATE 35. |
| K15 | * | * | | Her. s. 1634? | | | PLATE 35. |
| K16 | * | * | * | Her. s. 362 | | | *AE/NB* fig. omits horizontal lines between shields. PLATES 4, 27 and 35. *PM* I.694, fig. 516, III. 313, fig. 204. |

## L.  EAST TEMPLE REPOSITORY (here omitted as being an earlier deposit)

## M. CENTRAL SHRINE (B) (Plan at PLATE 1,19–20)

*AE/NB* 1901.26; *DM/DB* 1901, April 6.
*BSA* 7 (1900–1) 28–29, 9 (1902–3) 37, 39, 10 (1903–4) 28; *PM* I.159, 313, 464, II.334, 524, 761, 768, 800, 804, 808, 831, III.4, 414, 463, IV.18, 585, 596, 606–7, 611.

In the middle section of the Central Shrine, left unexcavated from the previous season, a small group of fragmentary seal-impressions came to light (PLATE 1,20); a stray sealing (M2) belonging to the same series was found on top of the wall 'to N. of this space' and another (M5) 'in chamber to W.' (*AE/NB* 1901.26) (PLATE 1,19). From a preliminary study of the nodules Evans thought he could discern two types, the variant factor being the position of the lions' forepaws, whether they rested on a mountain or on a base-line. More detailed examination while preparing the *BSA* report showed him that there was, after all, but one type involved, and that which he had first imagined to be a variant was the result of M4's abraded surface. In some of his later works Evans overlooked this correction, returning to his original misconception (*PM* II.808, IV.596).

| Ref. no. | Sketch | Description | Drawing | Sealing | Other examples | AE Cat. | Comments and plate reference |
|---|---|---|---|---|---|---|---|
| M1 | * | | * | Her. s. 166/2 | | B1 | PLATES 5, 27 and 36. |
| M2 | * | | * | Her. s. 141/1 | | | PLATES 27 and 36. |
| M3 | * | * | * | Her. s. 166/1,3 | | | PLATES 5, 27 and 36. |
| M4 | * | * | * | Her. s. 168/3 | | B2 | PLATES 27 and 36. |
| M5 | | * | * | Her. s. 141/2 | | B1 | 'upper part of attendant'. PLATES 5, 27 and 36. |

*Additional Table: PM* IV.602.

| AE Cat. | Ref. no. |
|---|---|
| B1 | M1–3 |
| | M5 |
| B2 | M4 |

## N. ROOM OF THE CHARIOT TABLETS (Plan at PLATE 1,24)

*AE/NB* 1900.22–25 *bis*, 27, 30, 42, 44–45; *DM/DB* 1900, April 12.
*BSA* 6 (1899–1900) 29; *SM* I.42; *PM* IV.593, n., 615, 669.
*OKT* 73–5, Pls. III, Va-c, VI, VIIa.

A sketch-plan of the Throne Room Area at the top of page 30 (*AE/NB* April 12) separates 'Three more seals ....' from a section on the previous page dealing with inscriptions on the Chariot tablets; the paragraph referring to these sealings contains no reference to provenance and is followed by a discussion of the Throne Room Area. Despite their apparent Throne Room context the sealings are rather to be associated with the Chariot Tablet deposit, for the sketch-map is arbitrarily placed, having been roughed out in pencil prior to any inked entries for the day, and *DM/DB* mentions sealings on the same day 'almost all of which have been found in the NE corner' (i.e. the Room of the Chariot Tablets). With the published description of N7 (*SM* I.42) Evans displays no doubts as to its provenance. Only two of the above sealings are sketched (N7, 8) and it is not clear whether '& part of another' following the description of N8 ('animal with its head turned back') refers still to that sealing, to another of the same type, or to a fragment bearing a different motif. Analogy with punctuation elsewhere in *AE/NB* and two lines in the right-hand quarter of the *AE/NB* figure make it more likely that part of a second animal was preserved on N8. In that case, to account for Evans's mention of 'lions' in the published list of motifs from the Room of the Chariot Tablets (*SM* I.42) (assuming the list to be accurate, the total of 14 sealings to be exact (*BSA* 6 (1899–1900) 29), and N13 to be one of this number), an otherwise unrecorded lion impression must be identified with the third sealing (N9). On the other hand the passage in *SM* I may have been composed only from a cursory examination of the Notebook and possibly F2 appearing on the same page as N6 was incorporated in the list. Evans thought that the defaced side of N12 may have borne a seal-impression, of which a few lines of the superimposed countermark survive. There is no comparable example at Knossos of such a long counter-signing as this would involve, whereas two other inscribed nodules without impressions do exist (Her. s. 125 (J4), 193 (G17)). N12 may have been similar to these. All the sealings in this deposit have fired to a shiny black. N13 is in the same condition and probably is part of the same deposit though it is not clear from the description, 'just S. of the Stone Vase room' (*AE/NB* 1900.45), whether it was found actually in the Room of the Chariot Tablets or further west. According to *SM* I.42 the sealing with chariot and riders was 'almost entirely destroyed by the conflagration'; in *PM* IV.615 the same object was 'insufficiently baked' and 'reduced to pulp by a sudden storm of heavy rain'. Whatever its fate, there is no trace of Na in either museum.

| Ref. no. | Sketch | Description | Drawing | Sealing | Other examples | AE Cat. | Comments and plate reference |
|---|---|---|---|---|---|---|---|
| N1 | * | * | | Her. s. 253 | | | PLATES 5 and 36. |
| N2 | * | * | | Her. s. 110 | | | *AE/NB* fig. omits base-line. PLATES 5 and 36. |
| N3 | | * | | | | | 'uncertain device. bit of palm tree'. PLATE 36. |
| N4 | | * | | | | | 'uncertain (?eagle)'. PLATE 36. |
| N5 | * | * | | | | | 'woman and shrine'. PLATE 36. |
| N6 | * | * | | Her. s. 111 | | | *AE/NB* fig. omits base-line and mistakes tail (? or stem of tree) for a back leg, one of which is missing from the edge of the nodule. PLATES 5 and 36. |
| N7 | * | * | | Her. s. 122 | | | PLATES 5, 27 and 37. |
| N8 | * | * | | | | | PLATE 37. |
| N9 | | * (?) | | | | | '& part of another' (?). Probably part of description of N8. PLATE 37. |
| N10 | * | * | | Her. s. 121 | | | *AE/NB* fig. back leg and tail confused. PLATES 5, 27 and 37. |
| N11 | * | * | | Her. s. 112 | | | PLATES 5 and 37. |
| N12 | * | * | | Her. s. 117 | | | Inscribed nodule without impression. |
| N13 | * | * | | Her. s. 124 | | | *AE/NB* fig. omits head of second animal behind first. PLATES 5, 27 and 37. |
| Na | | | | | *PM* IV.593 n. | | 'chariot and horses with the two riders'. |

## O. REST OF THE WEST WING

*Corridor of the Stone Basin* (Plan at PLATE 1,14)

*AE/NB* 1900.51.
*OKT* 111.

| Ref. no. | Sketch | Description | Drawing | Sealing | Other examples | AE Cat. | Comments and plate reference |
|---|---|---|---|---|---|---|---|
| O1 | * | * | | Her. s. 205 | | | clay matrix. PLATES 6 and 37. |

*Threshold between the Room of the Stone Bench and the Room of the Stone Drum* (Plan at PLATE 1,15)

> *AE/NB* 1901.17, 19.
> *BSA* 7 (1900–1) 32; *PM* IV.414, 925.

| Ref. no. | Sketch | Description | Drawing | Sealing | Other examples | AE Cat. | Comments and plate reference |
|---|---|---|---|---|---|---|---|
| O2 | * | * | * | Her. s. 133 | | | PLATES 6, 27 and 37. |

*Stepped Portico* (Steps ascending south of the Throne Room, East Portico) (Plan at PLATE 1,16)
> *AE/NB* 1900.56.

| Ref. no. | Sketch | Description | Drawing | Sealing | Other examples | AE Cat. | Comments and plate reference |
|---|---|---|---|---|---|---|---|
| O3 | * | * | | Her. s. 106 | | | PLATES 24 and 37. |

*Room of the Niche* (Plan at PLATE 1,21)

> *AE/NB* 1900.66, 69, 1901.17 *bis*; DM/DB 1900, May 8.
> *SM* I.42; *PM* IV.618.
> *OKT* 34, 82, pl. IXb.

A cross-wall divides the magazine into two unequal compartments; in the smaller, between the partition and a doorway leading south into the East Pillar Room, 3 impressions were found (*DM/DB* 1900, May 8), 4 according to *AE/NB*. O4 and O5 were drawn with the entry for May 8th (*AE/NB* 1900.66) but O6 was omitted and only sketched a few days later, erroneously associated with a clay label from Magazine 6 (*AE/NB* 1900.69). Correction and cross-reference to the deposit in the Room of the Niche appear to have been made almost immediately. The fourth was described as 'two bulls back to back'. An isolated entry in *AE/NB* 1901.17 *bis* notes a countermarked sealing (O7) from the '½ blocked entrance N. of Pillar Rooms', presumably the Room of the Niche. There is no evidence of further excavation here at that time and while the sealing(s) may have come to light during a general tidy-up of the site, more probably O7 is to be identified with the sealing described the previous season.

| Ref. no. | Sketch | Description | Drawing | Sealing | Other examples | AE Cat. | Comments and plate reference |
|---|---|---|---|---|---|---|---|
| O4 | * | * | * | Her. s. 108 | | | PLATES 6, 28 and 38. *SM* I.43, fig. 20a; *PM* IV.617, fig. 604a. |
| O5 | * | * | | Her. s. 118 | | | *AE/NB* fig. omits horns. PLATES 6 and 38. |
| O6 | * | * | | Her. s. 225 | | | PLATES 6 and 38. |
| O7 | * | * (?) | | Her. s. 156 | Her. s. 224 | | PLATES 6, 28 and 38. |

*Vat Room* (here omitted as being an earlier deposit)

*Corridor of the House Tablets* (Plan at PLATE 1,23)

> *AE/NB* 1900.51.

| Ref. no. | Sketch | Description | Drawing | Sealing | Other examples | AE Cat. | Comments and plate reference |
|---|---|---|---|---|---|---|---|
| O11 | * | * | | Her. s. 116 | | | PLATES 24 and 38. |

*Room of the Column Bases* (Plan at PLATE 1,22)

> *AE/HL* 1900.
> *BSA* 6 (1899–1900) 28.
> *OKT* 34.

In his article Evans comments on a deposit of clay tablets found in the north-east corner of the Room of the Column Bases together with remains of a gypsum chest and 'two of the clay seals with which the chest itself had been secured'. Although no mention is made of these sealings in *AE/NB*, they are listed with the associated tablets in the contemporary *AE/HL* and described as 'two clay seals with impression of seal representing four bulls' which permits certain identification. Their attribution to the Archives Deposit (C51) is erroneous.

| Ref. no. | Sketch | Description | Drawing | Sealing | Other examples | AE Cat. | Comments and plate reference |
|---|---|---|---|---|---|---|---|
| O12 | | * | * | Her. s. 139/1–2 | | | PLATES 6, 17 and 28 (C51). |

## Q. SOUTH-WEST BASEMENTS (A) (Plan at PLATE 1,25–27)

*AE/NB* 1901.16–17, 33 *bis* 34; *DM/DB* 1901, March 9, 14, 16, April 20, 22, 24–25.
*BSA* 7 (1900–1) 16–20; *PM* II.307, 762–8, 770–1, III.137, IV.387, 395, 512, 564, 570, 593–5, 601–2, 607, 615.
*OKT* 152–4.

Sealings excavated from a group of basement rooms to the south of the Central Court were mainly concentrated above floor level in the Room of the Seal Impressions, the Room of the Clay Signet (Room of the Priest Fresco, i.e. the Palanquin fresco, not the Priest-king relief), and the Room of the Egyptian Beans. The 'Lapidary's Workshop' was located by Evans in this latter room and the compartment immediately north of it (Room of the Wheat), but objects attributed to it came from a wider area. These include the sealings listed *PM* IV.594–5, whose allocation to the workshop seems to have been arbitrary, based presumably on a later consideration of style. There may have been sealings other than Q19–21 excavated from the Room of the Egyptian Beans; they may have carried such scenes as are described in *PM* IV (cf. *BSA* 7 (1900–1) 16), but the list itself is derived mainly from *AE/NB* 1901.16, as alterations in the Notebook reveals. Initially the entry under 'Notanda to Mar. 25' (*AE/NB* 1901.16–17) ascribed Q1–18 all to the Room of the Seal Impressions, but at a subsequent date (apparently some time between the composition of *PM* II and IV) the heading on the first side was deleted and replaced by 'Lapidary's Workshop', thus distinguishing Q1–7 from Q8–18 of the 'R. of Seal Impressions proper'. Curiously the 'Workshop' itself (i.e. the Room of the Egyptian Beans) was not excavated until the middle of April, nor were the sealings recorded by Evans from there (Q19–21) ever assigned to the 'Lapidary's Workshop'. A cross-reference (A7) to sealings from the Armoury Deposit as impressed by the same lentoid is not substantiated by existing material; of the several similarly contorted animals (Vc, d) none is identical to Q8. Possibly Q10, '2 goats, one head visible behind the other's back' is described in the published catalogue as 'couchant oxen heads in opposite positions' (A10). *AE/NB* fig. Q13 combines Her. s. 162 and Her. s. 1258, though they were certainly impressed by different sealstones. Q15 is from the same stone as Q17, the series of circles to the right of the impaled triangle being the horn of one of the animals. The design of Q17 is alternatively attributed to the South-West Basement Deposit (*PM* IV.570, fig. 544c, A8) and the Archives or East Hall Borders Deposit (*PM* IV.570, D21). Evans is positive about the existence of two sealings, D21 being the 'same as S.W. Basement Deposit' (*PM* IV.605). On the other hand only one more or less complete sealing has survived, and as the *AE/NB* sketch was cut from its page, a reduplication could have been produced if this, like other cuttings, was misplaced. Evans may then have included it, as well as the pencilled note that remains beside the gap in *AE/NB*, in his final *PM* IV catalogues. Q20 is accidentally ascribed to the Archives Deposit (*PM* IV.564). Apart from the similar impressions already accounted for in Section K, there are three and a half standing-bitch sealings. Whether they should be identified with the '3½ examples' from the Room of the Egyptian Beans (Q21) is problematic. Their condition (Her. s. 214–15: greyish-black, Ox. 1938. 1014b and d: red) does not conflict with such an identification since Q19–20 show an equal diversity of colour (Her. s. 160–1: brownish-black, Her. s. 143: red). On the other hand 'pieces' are also recorded from the Domestic Quarter (R53). If Evans literally meant that just fragments came from the Corridor beyond the Hall of the Colonnades, then they are among the group of sealings from this deposit still missing, and identification of Her. s. 214–15 etc. with those from the South-West Basement is fairly safe. But if whole standing-bitch sealings also occurred in the Corridor, then Her. s. 214–15 may belong to the Domestic Quarters Deposit, as the shape of the nodules, perforation and impression of basketry on their backs resemble other sealings from that part of the Palace (R1, 51, 54). Illustrations claiming to be Q22 (*PM* II.767, fig. 498, IV.395, fig. 331) in fact depict the composition reversed as on the sealings R1 etc. If only one sealing is involved, A5 is more likely to belong to the Archives Deposit. Nowhere mentioned in *AE/NB*, it was first published *PM* II.765 and assigned to the 'Treasury Deposit of the Domestic Quarters' in a section otherwise devoted to discussion of the S.W. Basement Deposit (cf. *PM* IV.610). Evans may have derived Catalogue A and the preliminary comments (*PM* IV.601, 594) from that earlier section, overlooking the qualifying remarks as to the provenance of A5. Three sealings from the Magazine of the Vase Tablets (K1, 2, and 4) 'dog ... lion leaping on lioness ... goddess and votary' (*BSA* 7 (1900–1) 18; *PM* II.764) were attributed to this deposit through an oversight (later corrected); Evans had failed to notice that the sealings sketched *AE/NB* 1901.17 were from various parts of the excavation. Similar dog impressions did however occur in the Room of the Egyptian Beans (Q21).

### Room of the Seal Impressions (Plan at PLATE 1,25)

| Ref. no. | Sketch | Description | Drawing | Sealing | Other examples | AE Cat. | Comments and plate reference |
|---|---|---|---|---|---|---|---|
| Q1 | * | * | | Her. s. 1230 | | | marking 2 examples. PLATES 6 and 38. |
| Q2 | * | | | Her. s. 1204/3 | Her. s. 1204/1–2 | | marking 11 examples. PLATES 6, 17 |
| | | * | | | Her. s. 1640 | | and 38. |
| Q3 | * | | | | Her. s. 1677–9 | | |
| Q4 | * | * | | Her. s. 1222 | | | PLATES 6 and 38. |
| Q5 | * | * | | | | | PLATES 6 (see notes) and 38. |
| Q6 | * | | | Her. s. 1226/2 | Her. s. 1226/1 | | *AE/NB* fig. omits one of the forelegs. PLATES 6, 17 and 38. |
| Q7 | * | * | | Her. s. 1207 | Her. s. 1217 | A9 | PLATES 6 and 38. |
| Q8 | * | * | | Her. s. 1246 | | A7 | PLATES 6 and 39. |
| Q9 | * | * | | Her. s. 1203 | | A12 | PLATES 6 and 39. |
| Q10 | * | * | | | | A10(?) | PLATE 39. |
| Q11 | | * | | Her. s. 1228(?) | | | 'Hindquarters of bull'.PLATE 39. cf. Q15. |
| Q12 | * | * | | Her. s. 1639 | | | PLATES 6 and 39. |
| Q13 | * | * | * | Her. s. 162 (Her. s. 1258) | | A13 | PLATES 6, 28 and 39 (2 types combined) |
| Q14 | * | * | * | Her. s. 134 | Her. s. 135 | A4 | PLATES 7, 28 and 39. |
| Q15 | * | | | Her. s. 1209 | Her. s. 1228 | | PLATES 7 and 39. cf. Q17. |
| Q16 | * | | * | Her. s. 360 | | A3 | PLATES 7, 28 and 39. |
| Q17 | * | | | | Ox. 1938. 1047 | A8 | PLATES 7, 28 and 39; Kenna 49S. cf. Q15, D21. |
| Q18 | * | * | | Her. s. 1303 | | A14 | PLATES 7 and 39. |

### Room of the Egyptian Beans (Plan at PLATE 1,27)

| Ref. no. | Sketch | Description | Drawing | Sealing | Other examples | AE Cat. | Comments and plate reference |
|---|---|---|---|---|---|---|---|
| Q19 | * | * | * | Her. s. 160 Her. s. 161 | | A2 | 'two'. PLATES 7, 28 and 39. |
| Q20 | * | * | * | Her. s. 143 | | A11 | PLATES 7, 28 and 39. |
| Q21 | | * | | Her. s. 214–15 ) Ox. 1938. 1014b,d) (?) | | A6 | '3½ examples'. PLATES 4, 27and 39. Kenna 40S. cf. K4. |

### Room of the Clay Signet (Plan at PLATE 1,26)

| Ref. no. | Sketch | Description | Drawing | Sealing | Other examples | AE Cat. | Comments and plate reference |
|---|---|---|---|---|---|---|---|
| Q22 | * | | | Her. s. 283 | | A1 | matrix. PLATES 7 and 40. |

### Additional Table: PM IV.601

| AE Cat. | Ref. no. | AE Cat. | Ref. no. | AE Cat. | Ref. no. |
|---|---|---|---|---|---|
| A1 | Q22 | A6 | Q21 | A11 | Q20 |
| A2 | Q19 | A7 | Q8 | A12 | Q9 |
| A3 | Q16 | A8 | Q17 | A13 | Q13 |
| A4 | Q14 | A9 | Q7 | A14 | Q18 |
| (A5) | Ca | A10 | Q10? | A15– | |

| Ref. no. | Comment |
|---|---|
| Aa | *PM* II.766 'other types … referring to bull-grappling scenes'. |
| Ab | *PM* IV.595 'goats'. |
| Ac | *PM* IV.595 'horned sheep and a section of a conventional palm tree'. |

### R.  EAST WING (Archives Deposit (C) and East Hall Borders Deposit (D)) (Plan at PLATE 1,29–38)

*AE/NB* 1901.34, 46–47, 1902.4–6, 31, 36, 38, 42–43, 45, 48–49, 51; *DM/DB* 1901, May 6, 11, 16, 18, 20, 27, June 1, 6, 1902, March 6, 8, 11, 17, 28, April 5, 8, 16, 18, 19, May 19.
   *BSA* 7 (1900–1) 29, 100–2, 105, 108, *BSA* 8 (1901–2) 38, 60, 67, 103, 109; *JHS* 45 (1925) 17; *PM* I.346, 682, 687, 695, 713, II.765, 767, III.219, 297, 302, 313, 316, 399, 404, 474, 488, IV. xviii, 343, 441, 451, 501, 520–1, 564, 578, 580, 593, 596–9, 602–4, 606, 607, 610, 614–15, 619, 627, 736, 956.
   *OKT* 137–148, pls. XXI-XXII.

The exact relation of sealing deposits to the original floors in this part of the palace is problematic. The destruction of the building, collapse of upper floors and staircases through conflagration and decay, and finally the weathering away of the superstructures have produced stratigraphical confusion. Sealings found on the Grand Staircase Landing level with the Upper East-West Corridor, and deposited from the collapse of a higher floor perhaps level with the Central Court, may once have been stored in the same archive or in one on the same floor as sealings that ended up in the Lower East-West Corridor. Even more difficult to assess is how great a depth those from the Wooden Staircase and neighbouring areas may have fallen from their original resting places. All that can now be determined with any certainty is the position of the sealings as excavated relative to the floor beneath them (and even here there is occasional ambiguity in the evidence).

From the surviving upper floor, Mackenzie, who as usual provides most of the details concerning circumstances of excavation, records sealings in the Upper East-West Corridor (*DM/DB* 1901, May 6; PLATE 1,36), the Landing (PLATE 1,34) and adjacent steps of the Grand Staircase (*DM/DB* 1901, May 11, 16, 18, 20) 'just above floor level', and 'on steps near the top' of the East-West Staircase at the other end of the Corridor (*DM/DB* 1901, June 6; PLATE 1,38). Collapse of the Wooden Staircase and associated upper floors deposited more nodules in a middle stratum, below the level of the Upper East-West Corridor but well above the ground floor (*DM/DB* 1901, May 27, June 1, 1902, April 18, 19; PLATE 1,32). According to *DM/DB* 1902, May 1, no sealing occurred below 'a line drawn from the base of the landing block 15 to landing block 16' i.e. about 1.40 metres from the floor. The motif on many sealings from the stairwell caused it to be called the Area of Daemon Seals, a name accidentally placed further west (*PM* III.404). R107 was evidently from the flight above the first landing on the Secret Staircase (PLATE 1,31), being recorded with other objects from the 'upper part' of the 'New Stairs' (*AE/NB* 1902.45). Two entries in *AE/NB* 1902 (pp. 31, 36) are a little enigmatic. The one records a sealing (R100) on March 1 from the 'Room of Stone Bed(?)' which is published as coming from near the Room of the Archives (*BSA* 8 (1901-2) 103), the other a sealing (R101) on March 6 from the 'High Seat R.'. Both probably refer to the Room of the Stone Bench, but to what level in this room or even below in the Room of the Plaster Couch, it is difficult to determine. In 1901 (*DM/DB* 1901, May 31, June 1, 17) the room had been almost entirely excavated down to floor level and below. Its next mention in *DM/DB* is not until the end of March 1902, three weeks after the sealings had turned up, the first possibly in the course of a general tidying of the site after the rain on February 28, the other when clearing was begun 'near doorway in N.W. Corner'. As a doorway had been marked in that position on Mackenzie's plans as early as May 27, 1901, Evans's remark on March 7, 1902 that a 'Door appears in N.W. corner of R. of Seat' leads one to suspect that the upper levels of the Room of the Plaster Couch were being excavated, despite the published attribution of a fresco fragment found with R101 to a position above the floor in the Room of the Stone Bench (*PM* III.297). Other sealings were found in the Lower East-West Corridor (*DM/DB* 1902, March 6, 11, 17; PLATE 1,37) some way above the floor (with the possible exception of those found on June 6, 1901 'at foot of the N. doorpost', though this reference may be to location rather than level; PLATE 1,35). Similarly, in the doorway leading south from the Hall of Colonnades and the passageway beyond (*DM/DB* 1902, March 28, April 5; PLATE 1,33) and in the Court of the Distaffs (*DM/DB* 1902, April 8), sealings are associated not with the floor deposit but with fallen debris. In the Treasury (*DM/DB* 1902, May 19) 'in the deposit on the floor between the S.E. and S.W. corners large numbers of seal impressions have been coming up' (PLATE 1,29). Further east, sealings were found embedded in rubble over the balustrade slabs of the lustral area in the Queen's Megaron (*AE/NB* 1902.38) and in the bathroom itself (*AE/NB* 1902.42, 43; PLATE 1,30).

Comparing the Notebooks, certain omissions from *AE/NB* are at once evident; not one of the sealings from the East-West Staircase (1901), Upper East-West Corridor (except for R1) (1901), Treasury, and Court of the Distaffs (1902) is mentioned, and neither Notebook refers to those in the corridor by the Treasury (*BSA* 8 (1901-2) 67-68). Of the sealings Evans has illustrated, the location of those excavated towards the end of the 1901 season and sketched on the early pages of *AE/NB* 1902 present the main problem. The entries on page 5, written, it seems, before those on page 4, started with a general heading 'E.W. Gallery S. of Gt. Tank system & below nr. E. door of Hall of Colonnades'; the alteration of this to read 'Gallery of Daemon Seals' was probably made when Evans, having filled the one side, wished to add a few more drawings on the page opposite, and noticing that he had as yet only recorded one of the sealings from the Lower East-West Corridor, decided to distinguish between the finds from the two areas. These additions from 'below Upper E.W. Corr.' he sketched at the bottom of page 4 (PLATE 43 left) beneath a horizontal line, extended across on to page 5 to include R52. Above the line is a further note 'below E.-W. passage. nr. E. door of Hall of Colonnades' with a downward pointing arrow, perhaps added for clarity when Evans drew six more sealings in the upper part of the page. Arrows here, above and below the central comment 'Hall of Colonnades', do not point to specific sealings and were probably meant to indicate that the whole group was part of the same deposit. The last entry is that at the top of page 4, a heading 'Part of Treasury Dep.' that could not have been made before 1902 and may have been written several years later. It is usually obvious when Evans is enumerating his sketches and when he is recording the number of specimens of a particular type. On *AE/NB* 1902.4 this distinction is not clear. The numerals 1–4 beside R46, 45, 49, 50 respectively could well indicate the number of examples, especially as 3 copies of R49 have survived and more than 4 of R50. Likewise the reason for labelling R40, 42 above the horizontal line, 1 and 2, is not apparent.

Inexact correspondence between the published division of sealings from the Domestic Quarters into Archives (C) and East Hall Borders (D) Deposits and the distribution of finds according to the Notebooks, may in part be due to Evans's separate compilation of C and D from *AE/NB* with the result that he has occasionally admitted the same sealing, or sealings from the same area, to both lists. Thus each catalogue includes sealings from the Grand Staircase landing, Lower East-West Corridor and (!) the Little Palace. This apparent overlapping may also be because of the incompleteness of the initial record and the surviving material; types recorded in one place may in fact have been common to several.

Sealings impressed with the same design as the matrix from the Room of the Clay Signet were found in various places in the Domestic Quarters; part of an impression came from the Upper East-West Corridor (R1), two from the Lower East-West Corridor (R51), and several from the Corridor leading south from the Hall of Colonnades (R54). Again there can be no absolute certainty about which of the existing sealings corresponds to those referred to in *AE/NB*, but Her. s. 281 is only a fragment and differs in colour and usage from the others (being a small greyish perforated lump), so may be R1. Her. s. 280 is also exceptional in being a large carbonized ball of clay perforated by a thick four-stranded cord, and may be one of R51, especially as Her. s. 252 (R43) is similar in shape and condition. Against this equation it might be argued that the intensity of heat to which that sealing was subjected was governed not by its position in the palace but by its usage. That similar balls of clay (Her. s. 212–13 (R6)) from another part of the Domestic Quarters and only sealings of this shape have suffered in the same way is surely more than coincidence. Sealings vary in shape according to usage and lumps of this form were probably attached to some highly inflammable material. Once touched by fire, whatever the intensity of the general blaze affecting other sealings in the vicinity, such balls would be subjected to a much fiercer local heat. The remainder of the 'goddess & cup' sealings are smaller red or black perforated nodules with impressions of basketry on their backs; these probably came from the Corridor south of the Hall of Colonnades (R54). A line round R8–9 (*AE/NB* 1901.46 *bis*) distinguishes them from the other sealings on the page as being found 'under blocking' at the entrance of the Corridor of the Bays, which would account for their omission from lists C and D (cf. *PM* I.682). The attribution of R50 to the same deposit (*PM* IV.521, n. 1) is a mistake if the *AE/NB* evidence has been interpreted correctly. Fragmentation of the nodules sometimes obscured for Evans the relationship between various parts of the same design. In one or two instances he sketched the parts separately as independent motifs, failing to notice for example that R12, 14, 27 all belong to the same picture of two hounds attacking their prey from above and divided from each other by an impaled triangle. *AE/NB* fig. R17 seems to combine two different seal-types, the basic design being Her. s. 230 with the heads added from Her. s. 232. The complete composition of which Her. s. 230 is a part (with Her. s. 231, 228, 210/ 1b,2 (R25, R29)) shows an upper row of crouching moufflons facing right divided from a similar row facing left by a horizontal bar that terminates in a *waz*-lily. The *AE/NB* sketch of R38 certainly looks like 'two lions confronted, in half-crouched positions, with bull's head between their heads' (i.e. C26) but both it and *PM* IV.609, fig. 597B,g (C50, 'Bull's head between two calves(?)') appear to depict Her. s. 367. This is probably a case of reduplicated publication of the same design whether or not a second sealing was involved. The description of R88 leaves no doubt as to identification with Her. s. 233 etc., though the only published mention of these sealings refers them to the Little Palace (cf. below E8).

The inclusion of C2 in the Archives Deposit was probably because of misidentification of a reference to a ritual scene (cf. above K2). C12 came from further north in the Court of the Stone Spout. From the *AE/NB* figure it is obvious how R84 came to be described as a 'boar to right, with tree behind' (C36), but no sketch nor sealing corresponds to C37 'boar walking right'. On the other hand there is an unpublished drawing which may have given rise to this description although the missing original was probably a seal. Similarly a drawing of a sealstone was the basis for C55. The only sealing corresponding to C48 is one from the Little Palace (U7) but there is no certainty whether Evans has made an error or is referring to an object which did derive from the Archives Deposit and has since been mislaid. Ca was listed in the South-West Basements Deposit but more likely belongs to the Archives (cf. above A5). Cd, Ce are noted in the Museum Catalogue as coming from this deposit, and string and basket-work impressions resembling those borne by R94 confirm the latter attribution; Her. s.663 on the other hand seems to correspond with U114. G11 and Q20 are accidentally ascribed to the Archives Deposit (*PM* IV.534, 564), E3 has been doubled as D3, and D21 may be a similar reduplication of Q17 (A8).

## *Upper East-West Corridor* (Plan at PLATE 1,36)

| Ref. no. | Sketch | Description | Drawing | Sealing | Other examples | AE Cat. | Comments and plate reference |
|---|---|---|---|---|---|---|---|
| R1 | | | * | Her. s. 281(?) | | D1 | 'part'. *AE/NB* 1901.34 note added to sketch of Q22. PLATES 17, 28 and 40; Kenna 41S, 42S. cf. R51, R54. |

## *Landing on Grand Staircase* (*AE/NB* 1901.46–47 *bis*) (Plan at PLATE 1,34)

| Ref. no. | Sketch | Description | Drawing | Sealing | Other examples | AE Cat. | Comments and plate reference |
|---|---|---|---|---|---|---|---|
| R2 | * | * | * | Her. s. 148 | | D8 | PLATES 8, 28 and 40. *BSA* 60 (1965) pl. 6. |
| R3 | * | | | Her. s. 289 | | D12? | PLATES 8 and 40. |
| R4 | * | * | | Her. s. 293 | | D15 | PLATES 8 and 40. |
| R5 | | * | | | | | 'Lower part of bull'. PLATE 40. |
| R6 | * | * | | Her. s. 212 Her. s. 1597 (Her. s. 1000) (Her. s. 1005) | Her. s. 213 | D10 | '3 examples', PLATES 8 and 40. |
| R7 | * | * | * | Her. s. 208 | | D6 | PLATES 8, 28 and 40. |
| R8 | * | * | * | Her. s. 250 | | | PLATES 8, 28 and 40. |
| R9 | * | | | Her. s. 251 | | | PLATES 8 and 41. |
| R10 | * | * | * | Her. s. 221 | | D13 C52 | PLATES 8, 28 and 41. |
| R11 | * | * | | Her. s. 1227 | | D14 | PLATES 9 and 41. |
| R12 | * | * | | Her. s. 305/1 | Her. s. 305/2 Her. s. 306–7 Her. s. 1625 | D23 | '4 + 1 examples', PLATES 9, 17, 25 and 41. cf. R14, R27. |
| R13 | * | * | * | Her. s. 211 | | | PLATES 9 and 41. *BSA* 60 (1965) pl. 6. |
| R14 | * | * | | Her. s. 314 | Her. s. 323–4 Her. s. 1237 | | '3', PLATES 9 and 41. cf. R12. |
| R15 | * | * | | Her. s. 222 | | D25 | 'bird flying' (*sic*) griffin. PLATES 9 and 41. |
| R16 | * | * | | Her. s. 364 | | D24 | PLATES 9 and 41. |
| R17 | * | * | | Her. s. 210/1a (Her. s. 232) | Her. s. 231 | | 2 types combined. PLATES 9, 25 and 41. cf. R25, R29. |
| R18 | * | * | | Her. s. 265 Her. s. 366 | Her. s. 275/7 Her. s. 365 | D16 | '3', PLATES 10, 25 and 41. |
| R19 | * | * | | Her. s. 294 | Her. s. 292/1,3–4 Her. s. 1234 | C18 | PLATES 10, 17, 25 and 41. cf. R30. |
| R20 | * | * | | Her. s. 1214 | | | PLATES 10 and 41. |
| R21 | * | * | | Her. s. 304 | | C30? | PLATES 10 and 41. |
| R22 | * | * | * | Her. s. 266 | | C61 | PLATES 10 and 41. *BSA* 60 (1965) pl. 6. |
| R23 | * | * | | Her. s. 303 | | C29 | PLATES 10 and 41. |
| R24 | * | * | | Her. s. 1643 | | | PLATES 10 and 41. |
| R25 | * | * | * | Her. s. 228 | | D19 | PLATES 9, 28 and 41. cf. R17. |
| R26 | * | * | | Her. s. 1188 | | | PLATES 10 and 41. |
| R27 | * | * | | Her. s. 300 Her. s. 301 | | | '2', PLATES 9 and 41. cf. R12. |
| R28 | * | * | | Her. s. 1235 | | D9? | *AE/NB* fig. omits the head turned back against the body. PLATES 10 and 41. |
| R29 | * | * | * | Her. s. 210/1b, 2 | | D22 | PLATES 9, 17, 25, 29 and 41. cf. R17. |
| R30 | * | * | | Her. s. 292/2 | | | PLATES 10 and 41. cf. R19. |
| R31 | * | * | | Her. s. 1646 | | | PLATES 10 and 41. |

| Ref. no. | Sketch | Description | Drawing | Sealing | Other examples | AE Cat. | Comments and plate reference |
|---|---|---|---|---|---|---|---|
| R32 | * | | * | Her. s. 158? | Her. s. 662 | C7/8<br>D2 | PLATES 10, 25, 29 and 42.<br>cf. *BSA* 60 (1965) pl. 5b. |
| R33 | * | * | | Her. s. 302 | | D16 | PLATES 10 and 42. |
| R34 | * | | | Her. s. 270 | | D17 | PLATES 11 and 42. |
| R35 | * | | | Her. s. 291 | | D7? | *AE/NB* fig. omits the man in front of the sphinx. PLATES 11 and 42. |
| R36 | * | | | Her. s. 229 | | | PLATES 11 and 42. |
| R37 | * | | | Her. s. 321 | | D18 | PLATES 11 and 42. |

## *Lower East-West Corridor* (*AE/NB* 1902.4–5) (Plan at PLATE 1,37)

| Ref. no. | Sketch | Description | Drawing | Sealing | Other examples | AE Cat. | Comments and plate reference |
|---|---|---|---|---|---|---|---|
| R38 | * | | * | Her. s. 367 | | C26<br>C50 | PLATES 11, 29 and 43. |
| R39 | * | * | | Her. s. 1029 | | C62 | PLATES 11 and 43. |
| R40 | | * | | | | | 'dog seizing agrimi'. PLATE 43. |
| R41 | * | * | | Her. s. 315 | | C24 | PLATES 11 and 43. |
| R42 | * | * | | Her. s. 310 | | C25 | PLATES 11 and 43. |
| R43 | * | | | Her. s. 252 | Her. s. 219–20 | D4 | '2', PLATES 11, 17, 25 and 43. |
| R44 | * | | | Her. s. 218 | | D5 | PLATES 11 and 43. |
| R45 | * | * | | Her. s. 1206/1 | Her. s. 1044<br>Her. s. 1206/2<br>Her. s. 1608 | D11 | '2', PLATES 11 and 43. |
| R46 | * | | | Her. s. 329 | Her. s. 1208 | | PLATES 11, 17 and 43. cf. K6. |
| R47 | * | * | | | | D20? | PLATE 43. |
| R48 | * | * | * | Her. s. 330/8 | Her. s. 330/9 | | PLATES 11 and 43. |
| R49 | * | * | | Her. s. 316–18 | | C17 | '3', PLATES 12, 25 and 43. |
| R50 | * | | * | Her. s. 242–5<br>Her. s. 268<br>Her. s. 274<br>Her. s. 1557–8 | | | '4', 5 rowers in each register.<br>PLATES 12, 25, 29 and 43. |
| R51 | | * | | Her. s. 280(?) | | C1 | 'two impressions of the signet with cup & orb'. PLATE 43. cf. R1. |
| R52 | * | * | | Her. s. 330/1–4<br>Her. s. 1247<br>Her. s. 1614 | | | '10', PLATES 12, 25 and 43. |

## *Doorway south from the Hall of the Colonnades and beyond* (*AE/NB* 1902.48–49) (Plan at PLATE 1,33)

| Ref. no. | Sketch | Description | Drawing | Sealing | Other examples | AE Cat. | Comments and plate reference |
|---|---|---|---|---|---|---|---|
| R53 | * | * | * | | | C38 | 'pieces', PLATES 27 and 42. cf. K4. |
| R54 | | * | * | Her. s. 277–9<br>Her. s. 282<br>Ox. s. 1938. 1015a–b | | C1 | 'several ... with the goddess & cup', cf. R1. PLATES 8, 17, 28 and 42. |
| R55 | * | * | | | | C47 | PLATE 42. |
| R56 | * | * | | | | | PLATE 42. |
| R57 | * | * | | Her. s. 1302? | Her. s. 1373 | | PLATES 12 and 42. |
| R58 | | * | | | | | 'parts of several animals'. PLATE 42. |
| R59 | * | | | Her. s. 309/6–7 | cf. Her. s. 1408,<br>Her. s. 1490,<br>Her. s. 1508,<br>Her. s. 1526/1–2 | C67 | 'several', a slightly smaller version of R83. PLATE 42. |
| R60 | * | * | * | Her. s. 260 | Her. s. 361 | C4 | '2', PLATES 12, 29 and 42. cf. R63. |
| R61 | * | * | * | Her. s. 267 | | C46 | PLATES 12, 29 and 42. |
| R62 | * | * | | | | C64 | PLATE 42. |
| R63 | * | | | Her. s. 271 | | C3 | PLATES 12 and 42. cf. R60. |
| R64 | * | * | | | | C59 | PLATE 42. |
| R65 | * | * | | | | C33 | 'several', PLATE 42. |
| R66 | * | * | * | Her. s. 272 | | C68 | PLATES 12, 29 and 42. |

## *Wooden Staircase* (*AE/NB* 1902.5–6) (Plan at PLATE 1,32)

| Ref. no. | Sketch | Description | Drawing | Sealing | Other examples | AE Cat. | Comments and plate reference |
|---|---|---|---|---|---|---|---|
| R67 | * | | | Her. s. 1197/1–2 | | | '2 + 1', PLATES 12 and 43. |
| R68 | | * | | Her. s. 1210<br>Her. s. 1361<br>Her. s. 1602<br>Her. s. 1606<br>Her. s. 1610 | | C52<br>D13 | 'Cow and calf similar to others (3) + 1 + 1', PLATE 43. cf. R10. |
| R69 | * | | | Her. s. 287 | | | PLATES 12 and 43. |
| R70 | * | * | | Her. s. 1238 | | C14 | PLATES 12 and 43. |
| R71 | * | * | | Her. s. 1229 | Her. s. 311/7 | C56 | '2', PLATES 12 and 43. |
| R72 | * | * | | | | C57 | PLATE 43. |

| Ref. no. | Sketch | Description | Drawing | Sealing | Other examples | AE Cat. | Comments and plate reference |
|---|---|---|---|---|---|---|---|
| R73 | * | | | Her. s. 1609 | | | PLATES 13 and 43. |
| R74 | * | * | | Her. s. 308/1–3 | Her. s. 1398 | C54 | PLATES 13, 25 and 43. cf. R97. |
| | | | | Her. s. 1257 | Her. s. 1518 | | |
| R75 | * | * | | Her. s. 1603 | | | PLATE 43. |
| R76 | * | * | | Her. s. 331–2 | | | '3', PLATES 13 and 43. |
| | | | | Her. s. 1604 | | | |
| R77 | * | * | | Her. s. 319 | | C32 | PLATES 13 and 43. |
| R78 | | * | | | | | 'parts of oxen (3)'. PLATE 43. |
| R79 | * | * | | Her. s. 320/1 | | | PLATES 13 and 43. |
| R80 | * | * | | Her. s. 1605 | | C22 | PLATES 13 and 43. |
| R81 | * | * | * | Her. s. 256/13 | | C13 | '18', PLATES 13, 17, 26, 29 and 43; |
| | | | | Her. s. 257/1–5 | | | Kenna 46S. |
| | | | | Her. s. 261–2 | | | |
| | | | | Her. s. 269 | | | |
| | | | | Her. s. 273 | | | |
| | | | | Her. s. 275/1–6 | | | |
| | | | | Her. s. 1365 | | | |
| | | | | Her. s. 1380 | | | |
| | | | | Ox. 1938. 1046 | | | |
| R82 | * | | | Her. s. 309/8 | | } C67 | '2', PLATE 43. |
| R83 | * | | | Her. s. 309/1–5 | | | '5 + 1', PLATES 13, 18, 26 and 43. cf. R59. |
| R84 | * | * | | Her. s. 311/1–2 | Her. s. 311/3–5 | C36 | 'boar 2' (sic) bull. PLATES 13 and 43. |
| | | | | | Her. s. 330/5–7,10 | | |
| R85 | * | * | | Her. s. 288 | | C58 | PLATES 14 and 42 |
| R86 | * | | | Her. s. 216 | | C49 | PLATES 14 and 42. |
| R87 | * | | | Her. s. 1617 | | | PLATES 14 and 42. |

## Wooden Staircase '& Secretaries' bureau' (AE/NB 1902.51) (Plan at PLATE 1,32)

| Ref. no. | Sketch | Description | Drawing | Sealing | Other examples | AE Cat. | Comments and plate reference |
|---|---|---|---|---|---|---|---|
| R88 | | * | * | Her. s. 233–8 | | E8 | 'two dogs or wolves & base very |
| | | | | Her. s. 256/1–12 | | | frequent'. PLATES 14, 18, 29 and 44. |
| | | | | Her. s. 1346 | | | |
| R89 | * | * | * | Her. s. 155 | | | PLATES 14, 29 and 44. |
| R90 | * | * | | | | C20 | PLATE 44. |
| R91 | * | * | * | Her. s. 157 | | | PLATES 14, 29 and 44. |
| R92 | * | * | * | Her. s. 163 | | C16 | PLATES 14, 29 and 44. |
| R93 | * | * | | | | } { C65 | PLATE 44. |
| R94 | * | * | | Ox. 1938. 947a-b | | } { C66 | PLATES 14, 26, 29 and 44. |
| | | | | | | | Kenna 47S, 48S. |
| R95 | * | * | | | | C31 | 'several', PLATE 44. |
| R96 | * | * | | | Her. s. 1036 (?) | C34 | 'several', PLATES 14 and 44. |
| R97 | * | * | | Her. s. 311/6 | | C39 | PLATES 13 and 44, cf. R74. |
| R98 | | * | | | | C44 | 'bull looking back & spray'. PLATE 44. |
| R99 | * | * | | | | C35 | PLATE 44. |

## Room of the Stone Bench (AE/NB 1902.31, 36) (Plan at PLATE 1,39)

| Ref. no. | Sketch | Description | Drawing | Sealing | Other examples | AE Cat. | Comments and plate reference |
|---|---|---|---|---|---|---|---|
| R100 | * | * | * | Her. s. 264 | | C21 | PLATES 14, 29 and 44. |
| R101 | * | | * | Her. s. 665 | | C40 | PLATES 14, 29 and 44. |

## Queen's Megaron (AE/NB 1902.38, 42, 43) (Plan at PLATE 1,30)

| Ref. no. | Sketch | Description | Drawing | Sealing | Other examples | AE Cat. | Comments and plate reference |
|---|---|---|---|---|---|---|---|
| R102 | * | * | * | Her. s. 153 | Her. s. 154 | C19 | PLATES 15, 29 and 44. |
| R103 | * | * | | Her. s. 226 | Her. s. 227 | C23 | PLATES 15, 26 and 44. |
| R104 | * | * | | | | C5 | PLATE 44. |
| R105 | * | * | | Her. s. 1189 | | C63 | PLATES 15 and 44. |
| R106 | * | * | | Her. s. 1183 | | | PLATES 15 and 45. |

## Secret Staircase (AE/NB 1902.45) (Plan at PLATE 1,31)

| Ref. no. | Sketch | Description | Drawing | Sealing | Other examples | AE Cat. | Comments and plate reference |
|---|---|---|---|---|---|---|---|
| R107 | * | * | | Her. s. 1691 | | C53 | PLATE 45. |

## Additional Table: PM IV.602.

| AE Cat. | Ref. no. | Sealing | Comment |
|---|---|---|---|
| C1 | R51, R54 | | cf. D1. |
| (C2) | K2 | | |

| AE Cat. | Ref. no. | Sealing | Comment |
|---|---|---|---|
| C3 | R63 | | |
| C4 | R60 | | |
| C5 | R104 | | |
| C6 | | | |
| C7 C8 | R32 | | cf. D2. |
| C9 | | Her. s. 669 | Drawing PLATES 15 and 30. |
| C10 | | Her. s. 668 | Drawing PLATES 15 and 30. |
| C11 | | Her. s. 664/1–2 | Drawing PLATES 15, 26 and 30. |
| (C12) | S6 | | |
| C13 | R81 | | |
| C14 | R70 | | |
| C15 | | Her. s. 259 | Drawing PLATES 15 and 30. |
| C16 | R92 | | |
| C17 | R49 | | |
| C18 | R19 | | |
| C19 | R102 | | |
| C20 | R90 | | |
| C21 | R100 | | |
| C22 | R80 | | |
| C23 | R103 | | |
| C24 | R41 | | |
| C25 | R42 | | |
| C26 | R38 | | cf. C50. |
| C27 C28 | R18? | | cf. D16. |
| C29 | R23 | | |
| C30 | R21? | | |
| C31 | R95 | | |
| C32 | R77 | | |
| C33 | R65 | | |
| C34 | R96 | | |
| C35 | R99 | | |
| C36 | R84 | | |
| (C37) | | | A seal? cf. *BSA* 60 (1965) pl. 5c. |
| C38 | R53 | | |
| C39 | R97 | | |
| C40 | R101 | | |
| C41 | | | Drawing PLATE 30. |
| C42 | | | Drawing PLATE 30. |
| C43 | | Her. s. 670 | Drawing PLATES 15 and 30. |
| C44 | R98 | | |
| C45 | | | Drawing PLATE 30. |
| C46 | R61 | | |
| C47 | R55 | | |
| (C48) | U7 | | cf. E22. |
| C49 | R86 | | |
| C50 | R38 | | cf. C26. |
| (C51) | O12 | | |
| C52 | R68 | | cf. D13. |
| C53 | R107 | | |
| C54 | R74 | | |
| (C55) | | Ox. 1941. 246 | A seal. *PM* III.317, fig. 209; Kenna 7P. |
| C56 | R71 | | |
| C57 | R72 | | |
| C58 | R85 | | |
| C59 | R64 | | |
| C60 | | Her. s. 667 | Drawing PLATES 15 and 30. |
| C61 | R22 | | |
| C62 | R39 | | |
| C63 | R105 | | |
| C64 | R62 | | |
| C65 C66 | R93 R94 | | |
| C67 | R59, R82–83 | | |
| C68 | R66 | | |
| Ca | | Her. s. 382 | PLATES 15 and 30. cf. A5. |
| Cb | | Her. s. 661 | PLATES 15 and 30. |
| Cc | | Her. s. 392 | PLATES 15 and 30. |
| (Cd) | | Her. s. 663 | cf. U114. |
| Ce | | Her. s. 671/1–4 Ox. n. No.8 | PLATE 24. |
| D1 | R1 | | cf. C1. |
| D2 | R32 | | cf. C7/8. |
| (D3) | U2 | | cf. E3. |

| AE Cat. | Ref. no. | Sealing | Comment |
|---------|----------|---------|---------|
| D4 ⎱ | ⎰ R43 | | |
| D5 ⎰ | ⎱ R44 | | |
| D6 | R7 | | |
| D7 | R35? | | |
| D8 | R2 | | |
| D9 | R28? | | |
| D10 | R6 | | |
| D11 | R45 | | |
| D12 | R3? | | |
| D13 | R68 | | cf. C52. |
| D14 | R11 | | |
| D15 | R4 | | |
| D16 | R33 | | |
| D17 | R34 | | |
| D18 | R37 | | |
| D19 | R25 | | |
| D20 | R47? | | |
| (D21) | Q17 | | cf. A8. |
| D22 | R29 | | |
| D23 | R12 | | |
| D24 | R16 | | |
| D25 | R15 | | |

## S. REST OF THE EAST WING

*Corridor of the Sword Tablets* (Plan at PLATE 1,28)

> *AE/NB* 1902.34.
> *BSA* 8 (1901–2) 94; *PM* II.331, IV.618, 853.
> *OKT* pl. XXIII.

It is not clear from *AE/NB* 1902.34 how many sealings are mentioned in a passage reading 'Also impression*s*(?) kneeling bull. & head'. If 'impression' is in the plural, does '& head' describe a third sealing from the Corridor? If so, is it the head of a man or a bull? The original sealing S1 has been mislaid but as far as can be seen from the photograph (*SM* II.pl. 88) it was impressed by the same lentoid as Vc.

| Ref. no. | Sketch | Description | Drawing | Sealing | Other examples | AE Cat. | Comments and plate reference |
|----------|--------|-------------|---------|---------|----------------|---------|------------------------------|
| S1 | * | * | | | | | PLATES 16 and 45, cf. Vc. |
| S2 | | * | | | | | 'kneeling bull', PLATE 45. |
| S3? | | * | | | | | '& head'. |

*Kapheneion* (Rubbish heap on south-east border of Palace) (here omitted as being an earlier deposit)

*Court of the Stone Spout* (Area of the Cowboy Fresco) (here omitted as being an earlier deposit)

## T.  EARLY PALACE DEPOSITS IN EAST (here omitted as being an earlier deposit)

## U. LITTLE PALACE (House of the Fetishes) (E) (Plan at FIG. I)

> *AE/NB* 1905.5–6, 9–11; *DM/DB* 1905, April 25, May 2, 3–20.
> *BSA* 9 (1904–5) 12–13, 16; *PM* I.683, 706, II.243–4, 523–4, 789, III.68, 316, IV.150–1, 387, 490, 534, 599–600, 605–7, 610, 612, 626–7, 827–8, 885.
> *OKT* 164–7, pls. XXVI-XXVIII.

Sketch-plans in *DM/DB* 1905 show a widespread distribution of sealings in the central part of the Little Palace, on both flights of the main staircase (FIG. I, 1–2), in the Room of the Fetish (FIG. I, 8) and neighbouring rooms to the west (FIG. I, 7), south-west (FIG. I, 4), and south (FIG. I, 5), as well as an overflow into the Hall of the Peristyle (FIG. I, 6) adjacent to the latter room, and in the Lustral Area (both Fetish Shrine (FIG. I, 9) and Corridor (FIG. I, 10)). In the various rooms Mackenzie comments on the 'loose tawny deposit' containing the impressions and the considerable height of these above the floor, but he does not describe the excavation of the sealings from the staircase, and in other respects his account is incomplete. In 1905 entries in *DM/DB* are irregular, referring sometimes to the activities of one day, sometimes to the work of a week or more; in the latter case certain details are bound to have been overlooked. On May 2, when recording the sealings that had so far

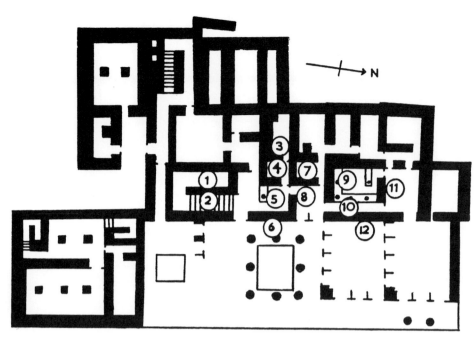

FIG. 1. PLAN OF THE LITTLE PALACE. (U)

1.⎫
2.⎭ Main Staircase

3. Cup Room
4. Room South-West of the Room of
   the Fetish

5. Room South of the Room of the
   Fetish
6. Hall of the Peristyle
7. Room West of the Room of the
   Fetish

8. Room of the Fetish
9. Lustral Area
10. 'Corridor by Shrine'
11. 'Room North of Shrine'
12. Megaron

come to light in FIG. I, 1–2, 4–8, Mackenzie noted that the Cup Room (FIG. I, 3) had not yet been completely excavated; as his next entry covers the period May 3–20, the omission of two sealings from the east end of this room is not surprising. Evans lists impressions also in the 'R. N. of Shrine' (FIG. I, 11), 'Stair N. landing' and the 'Megaron' (FIG. I, 12), presumably somewhere along the west wall. Some of his terminology is obscure. Nothing quite corresponds to the 'door W. of Shrine N.S. room'. The 'R. W. of Megaron? balustrade' apparently refers to FIG. I, 10, and is certainly regarded as such in Evans's later notes. Another entry is complicated by corrections and counter-corrections: 'S. Room r. S[E] of 'Fetish' [Shrine] 2. bordering Colonnade (from Stairs)' (FIG. I, 5); 'S' was probably an immediate substitution for 'E', while 'Shrine' seems to have been added and removed again at some later date. Because of the compressed arrangement of pages in *AE/NB* it is not always quite clear to how many of the surrounding sketches comments about location apply; they are probably as follows: 'Under door W. of Shrine N.S. Room' U2; (FIG. I, 1–2) 'Stairs' U25–26, 30–33, 'Stair. N. Landing' U34–52; (FIG. I, 3) 'E. end of Cup room' U28–29; (FIG. I, 8) 'R. of large fetish' U53–66; (FIG. I, 12) 'Megaron' U68–74; (FIG. I, 10) 'Corridor by Shrine' U75–79; (FIG. I, 7?) 'R. S. of Shrine' U80–83, 107; 'R.W. of Megaron? balustrade' U84–92; (FIG. I, 5) 'S. Room, r. S. of Fetish …' U93–106; (FIG. I, 11) 'R.N. of Shrine' U108–16. An odd page of later notes based on *AE/NB* adds only one detail, a reference to U117; other differences are few, the result of miscopying or misinterpretation of the earlier record by which for example U56, 64, 66–67 from FIG. I, 8 have been attributed to FIG. I, 9, and U80–83 from FIG. I, 7 to FIG. I, 10.

Study of the Little Palace Deposit is hampered by the large number of sealings still missing, so that few identifications are possible. It is difficult to decide whether U1 is an independent design or an abandoned attempt to sketch U2. In *PM* IV.387 this latter is correctly described and attributed to the Little Palace, while page 604 inaccurately lists it as D3. Another description of the same sealing (605 E3) differs considerably, being based on the *AE/NB* diagram rather than a re-examination of the original sealing or the figure drawn for publication. As neither seal nor impression is identifiable with U44 it is impossible to judge whether or not the comment 'steatite seal' applies to the 'two ducks'. Four designs catalogued as sealings from the Little Palace are in fact sealstones. Unpublished drawings exist of E5 and E7 as well as the published illustrations of E13 and Ea, so these may have been the source of the error. Despite the differences in position of the heads in Evans's sketch (G10) and the published illustration of Eb, both delineate the same sealing (Her. s. 209). This seems to be a case of mistaken attribution rather than an example of seal-types common to two deposits. The Notebooks leave no doubt that sealings with heraldic dogs either side of a concave base came from the Domestic Quarters, although none is published from there. The problem is whether similar ones (E8) came from the Little Palace. In *AE/NB* 1905.11 an asterisk and '2 dogs?' accompany the sketch of U101, which is published as E35 'two crouched dogs(?) confronted'. Though asterisks usually imply that an object is of such importance as to be specially drawn, U101 like U54 apparently was not. When studying his notebooks later Evans may have dissociated the description from the sketch, assuming a drawing to exist, and so identified R88 as coming from the Little Palace. The Herakleion Catalogue numbers exclude the possibility of any of the extant dog sealings belonging to that deposit, and from the sketch one cannot ascertain whether U18 came from the same seal or was merely a similar design. The catalogue number Her. s. 369 indicates that Ec was unearthed during the first four years of the Knossos excavation so for the same reason it cannot have come from the Little Palace. A part of the same design (Her. s. 1275) turned up in one of the stray boxes of impressions from the Main Palace (cf. PLATE 32(b)). Evidence for and against attributing Her. s. 663 to the Archives or Little Palace Deposit is practically equal; if anything, more in favour of the latter. Evans himself may have been uncertain when it came to publishing the lists of sealings in *PM* IV, since he catalogues it neither in Section C nor in Section E and mentions it in *PM* IV.607 (608, fig. 597 A,*h*) without reference to the findplace. An asterisk beside U114 shows that Evans had already had (or intended having) the 'man & lions looking away' drawn. Her. s. 663 is the only drawing to correspond to this description but an entry made in the Museum Catalogue notes Her. s. 663 as coming from the Treasury of the Domestic Quarters. Between 1922 when the box of sealings was found in the pottery stores and 1940 when these and others, unstratified and from the Little Palace, turned up again in one of the museum drawers, there had been plenty of opportunity for contents of different packets to become confused. Her. s. 663 could well have come from the Little Palace despite the remarks in the Museum Catalogue. Her. s. 650–60 appear to have been entered in the catalogue as a group; they had been separated from the other Knossos sealings to be drawn for publication, and were afterwards mislaid. The majority are identifiable as being from the Little Palace, which suggests that all may have been from the same source. The only difficulty with this supposition is that a sealing whose catalogue number Her. s. 353 excludes it from the Little Palace excavations was impressed by the same seal as Her. s. 660. In theory there is no reason why similar sealings should not have occurred in both palaces but as evidence for this is lacking it would be unwise to assume Her. s. 660 to derive from the Little Palace, especially in view of the time-lag mentioned above between entry into the museum (probably in 1922) and entry into the catalogue (1940). An accidental switching of boxes may well have affected Her. s. 660 (PLATES 21 and 26) as well as Her. s. 663.

| Ref. no. | Sketch | Description | Drawing | Sealing | Other examples | AE Cat. | Comments and plate reference |
|---|---|---|---|---|---|---|---|
| U1? | * | | | | | | PLATE 45. |
| U2 | * | | * | Her. s. 421 | | E3 | PLATES 16, 30 and 45. cf. D3. |
| U3 | * | * | | | | | PLATE 45. |
| U4 | * | * | | | | | PLATE 45. |
| U5 | * | | | | | | PLATE 45. |
| U6 | * | * | | | | | PLATE 45. |
| U7 | * | * | * | Her. s. 424 | | E22 | PLATES 16, 30 and 45. cf. C48. |
| U8 | * | * | | | | | PLATE 45. |
| U9 | | * | | | | | 'Forepart of running bull (good)', PLATE 45. |
| U10 | | * | | | | | 'Lion standing (rough)', PLATE 45. |
| U11 | | * | | | | | 'Back part of lion', PLATE 45. |
| U12 | * | | * | Her. s. 423 | | | PLATES 16, 30 and 45. |
| U13 | * | * | | | | | PLATE 45. |
| U14 | | * | | | | | 'Agrimi & young above. fair', PLATE 45. |
| U15 | | * | | | | | 'Agrimi & branch looking back (poor)', PLATE 45. |
| U16 | | * | | | | | 'Agrimi – shield below – '(poor)', PLATE 45. |
| U17 | | * | | | | | 'Bull? looking back – branch below (rough)', PLATE 45. |
| U18 | * | * | | | | | PLATE 45. |
| U19 | * | | * | Her. s. 422 | | | PLATES 16, 30 and 46. |

| Ref. no. | Sketch | Description | Drawing | Sealing | Other examples | AE Cat. | Comments and plate reference |
|---|---|---|---|---|---|---|---|
| U20 | * | * | | | | E18 | PLATE 46. |
| U21 | * | * | | | | E6 | PLATE 46. |
| U22 | * | * | | | | E30 | PLATE 46. |
| U23 | * | * | | | | E32 | PLATE 46. |
| U24 | * | * | | | | E37 | PLATE 46. |
| U25 | * | * | | | | | PLATE 46. |
| U26 | * | * | | | | | PLATE 46. |
| U27 | | * | | | | | 'Fragment. animals', PLATE 46. |
| U28 | * | * | | | | E24 | PLATE 46. |
| U29 | * | * | | | | E36 | PLATE 46. |
| U30 | * | * | | | | E28 | PLATE 46. |
| U31 | | * | * | Her. s. 651 | | | 'Man & lion (½) drawn', PLATES 16, 31 and 46. |
| U32 | * | * | | | | E29 | PLATE 46. |
| U33 | | * | | | | | 'animal fragments (2)', PLATE 46. |
| U34 | * | * | | | | E25 | PLATE 46. |
| U35 | * | * | | | | E27 | PLATE 46. |
| U36 | | * | | | | | 'forepart of lion (frag.)', PLATE 46. |
| U37 | * | * | | | | E17 | PLATE 46. |
| U38 | * | * | | | | | PLATE 46. |
| U39 | | * | | | | | 'Pt. of seated bull l.', PLATE 46. |
| U40 | | * | | | | E31 | 'Pt. of cow & calf', PLATE 46. |
| U41 | | * | | | | | 'hindquarters of standing bull', PLATE 46. |
| U42 | | * | | | | E33 | 'Two seated bulls reversed', PLATE 46. |
| U43 | * | * | | | | E40 | PLATE 46. |
| (U44) | * | * | | | | E41 | PLATE 46. |
| U45 | * | * | | | | | PLATE 46. |
| U46 | * | * | | | | | PLATE 46. |
| U47 | | * | | | | E38 | 'Animals with †'. † (impaled triangle), PLATE 46. |
| U48 | | * | | | | | 'Pt. of lion', PLATE 46. |
| U49 | | * | | | | | 'Pt. of standing bull', PLATE 46. |
| U50 | | * | | | | | 'Pt. of bull facing', PLATE 46. |
| U51 | | * | | | | | 'Pt. of agrimi running', PLATE 46. |
| U52 | | * | | | | | 'Pts. of animals various 6', PLATE 46. |
| U53 | * | * | | | | | 'fragments. 2', PLATE 47. |
| U54 | * | | * | Her. s. 659 | | E4 | PLATES 16, 31 and 47. |
| U55 | * | * | | | | | PLATE 47. |
| U56 | * | | * | Her. s. 418 | | E1 | PLATES 16, 31 and 47. |
| U57 | * | | | | | | PLATE 47. |
| U58 | | * | | | | | 'Agrimi seated looking back', PLATE 47. |
| U59 | | * | | | | | 'Animals? group of 4 back to back', PLATE 47. |
| U60 | | * | | | | | 'hindquarters bull', PLATE 47. |
| U61 | | * | | | | | 'bull l.', PLATE 47. |
| U62 | * | * | | | | E26 | '2. fragments do. l, l, l', PLATE 47. cf. U75, U87. |
| U63 | * | | | | | | PLATE 47. |
| U64 | * | * | | | | | PLATE 47. |
| U65 | | * | | | | | 'Animal fragments various. 4', PLATE 47. |
| U66 | | * | * | Her. s. 658 | | | 'Griffin (drawn)', PLATES 16, 31 and 47. cf. U71. |
| U67 | | * | | | | | 'Bull's head and † (drawn)', † (figure-of-8 shield), PLATES 31 and 47. |
| U68 | | * | | | | | 'Bull [head turned back] small', PLATE 47. |
| U69 | * | * | | | | | PLATE 47. |
| U70 | | * | | | | | 'Lion and prey (frag)', PLATE 47. |
| U71 | | * | | | | | 'Griffins as above', PLATE 47. cf. U66. |
| U72 | | * | | | | | 'Animals uncertain frags. 4', PLATE 47. |
| U73 | * | * | | | ?Her. s. 1045 | E23 | '2 frags.', PLATES 22 and 47. |
| U74 | * | | | | | | PLATE 47. |
| U75 | | * | | | | | 'Lion & palm as above', PLATE 47. cf. U62. |
| U76 | | * | | | | | 'Bull with head drawn back frag.', PLATE 47. |
| U77 | | * | | | | | 'Agrimi seated. 2', PLATE 47. |
| U78 | | * | | | | | 'Animal frags. 6', PLATE 47. |
| U79 | | * | | | | | 'Taurokathapsia frag. (ram's head) & forelegs of bull' = U73(?), PLATE 47. |
| U80 | | * | | | | | '2 animals galloping l. hind-quarters only', PLATE 47. |

| Ref. no. | Sketch | Description | Drawing | Sealing | Other examples | AE Cat. | Comments and plate reference |
|---|---|---|---|---|---|---|---|
| U81 | | * | | | | | 'Moufflons', PLATE 47. |
| U82 | | * | | | | | 'Part of lion & prey', PLATE 47. |
| U83 | | * | | | | | 'Agrimi group frag.', PLATE 47. |
| U84 | | * | | | | | 'Part of lion & prey', PLATE 47. |
| U85 | | * | | | | | 'Animals symmetrically grouped (4)', PLATE 47. |
| U86 | * | * | * | | | E10 | PLATES 31 and 47. |
| U87 | | * | | | | | 'fragment of lion (2)', PLATE 47. cf. U62, |
| U88 | | * | | | | | 'Animal frags. various. 8'. PLATE 47. |
| U89 | * | * | | | | E20 | PLATE 47. |
| U90 | | * | | | | | 'frag. with facing bull's head', PLATE 47. |
| U91 | | * | | | | | 'Part of agrimi', PLATE 47. |
| U92 | * | * | | | | E12 | PLATES 31 and 47. |
| U93 | * | | | | | E15 | PLATE 47. |
| U94 | | * | | | | | 'bull seated. 3', PLATE 47. |
| U95 | * | * | | | | | PLATE 47. |
| U96 | | * | | | | | 'Ox standing l.', PLATE 47. |
| U97 | | * | | | | | '-r.' (i.e. Ox standing right), PLATE 47. |
| U98 | * | * | | | | E39 | PLATE 47. |
| U99 | * | * | | | | | PLATE 47. |
| U100 | | * | | | | | 'Agrimia. frag.', PLATE 47. |
| U101 | * | * | | | | E35 | PLATE 47. |
| U102 | * | * | | | | E14 | PLATE 47. |
| U103 | | * | | | | | 'Animals various frag. 5', PLATE 47. |
| U104 | | * | | Her. s. 652 | | | 'Man & 2 lions', PLATES 16, 31 and 47. |
| U105 | | * | | Her. s. 657 | | | 'hieroglyphs', PLATES 24, 31 and 47. |
| U106 | | * | | Her. s. 654 | | E11 | 'facing head & 00', PLATES 16, 31 and 47. |
| U107 | * | * | | Her. s. 419 | | E2 | PLATES 16, 31 and 47. |
| U108 | * | * | | | | | '2', PLATE 47. |
| U109 | * | * | | | | | PLATE 47. |
| U110 | | * | | | | | 'Agrimia', PLATE 47. |
| U111 | * | * | | | | E21 | PLATE 47. |
| U112 | * | * | | Her. s. 417 | Her. s. 1269 | E16 | PLATES 16, 31 and 47. |
| U113 | | * | | | | | 'Agrimi? hindquarters', PLATE 47. |
| U114 | | * | | Her. s. 663 | | | 'Man & lions looking away', PLATES 16, 31 and 47. |
| U115 | | * | | Her. s. 656 | | | 'bull's head and O', PLATES 16, 31 and 47. |
| U116 | * | * | | | | E9 | PLATE 47. |

## Additional Table: PM IV.605–6.

| AE Cat. | Ref. no. | Sealing | Comment |
|---|---|---|---|
| E1 | U56 | | |
| E2 | U107 | | |
| E3 | U2 | | cf. D3. |
| E4 | U54 | | |
| (E5) | | Her. 838 | a seal. |
| E6 | U21 | | |
| (E7) | | | cf. Bossert, fig. 397 d. |
| (E8) | R88 | | |
| E9 | U116 | | |
| E10 | U86 | | |
| E11 | U106 | | |
| E12 | U92 | | |
| (E13) | | Her. 845 | a seal. PM IV.151, fig. 116. |
| E14 | U102 | | |
| E15 | U93 | | |
| E16 | U112 | | |
| E17 | U37 | | |
| E18 | U20 | | |
| E19 | | | PM IV.609, fig. 597 B, b. |
| E20 | U89 | | |
| E21 | U111 | | |
| E22 | U7 | | cf. C48. |
| E23 | U73 | | |
| E24 | U28 | | |
| E25 | U34 | | |
| E26 | U62 | | |
| E27 | U35 | | |
| E28 | U30 | | |
| E29 | U32 | | |
| E30 | U22 | | |
| E31 | U40 | | |

| AE Cat. | Ref. no. | Sealing | Comment |
|---------|----------|---------|---------|
| E32 | U23 | | |
| E33 | U42 | | |
| E34 | | | |
| E35 | U101 | | |
| E36 | U29 | | |
| E37 | U24 | | |
| E38 | U47 | | |
| E39 | U98 | | |
| E40 | U43 | | |
| (E41) | U44 | | Probably a seal. |
| E42 | | | |
| (Ea) | | Her. 840 | a seal. *PM* I.705, fig. 529 *d*, II.789, fig. 515, IV.490, fig. 421. |
| (Eb) | | | *PM* IV.535, fig. 486. cf. G10. |
| (Ec) | | Her. s. 369 | PLATES 20, 23, 31 and 32(b). |
| | | Her. s. 1275 | |
| Ed | | | *PM* IV.828, fig. 809. |

## V. OTHER DEPOSITS OUTSIDE MAIN PALACE

*Arsenal Deposit*

> *AE/NB* N.D. v.3; *DM/DB* 1904.84, 86, 88 *bis*.
> *BSA* 10 (1903–4) 55, 57, 60–62; *SM* I.44; *PM* III.116, IV.493, 615–18, 836.
> *OKT* 158, pl. XXV.

Evans distinguished three types of sealing from the Arsenal (*BSA* 10 (1904–5) 60 fig. 22 A, B and C), which he believed were all impressed by the same lion seal as a countermarked sealing from the Corridor of the Sword Tablets (S1). In fact two different seals were involved: Vc was responsible for types A, B and S1, and Vd for type C.

| Ref. no. | Sealing | | Comment and plate reference |
|----------|---------|--|----------------------------|
| Va | Her. s. 377/1–3 | | PLATES 16, 18 and 31; Kenna 51S. |
| | Ox. 1938. 1068 | | |
| Vb | Her. s. 375 | | PLATES 16 and 31. |
| Vc | Her. s. 119 | A | PLATES 16, 18 and 31; cf. S1. |
| | Her. s. 401 | | |
| | Her. s. 403 | B | |
| Vd | Her. s. 400/1–3 | C | PLATES 16, 18 and 31. |
| | Her. s. 402? | | |
| | Her. s. 1024 | | |
| | Her. s. 1600 | | |

*North-East House* (here omitted as being an earlier deposit)

*Royal Tomb, Isopata*

> *AE/NB* (N.D.v.3); *DM/DB* 1904 April 19.
> *PreT* II.141, 154 fig. 138.

| Ref. no. | Sketch | Description | Drawing | Sealing | Other examples | AE Cat. | Comments and plate reference |
|----------|--------|-------------|---------|---------|----------------|---------|------------------------------|
| V1 | * | * | | Her. s. 415/1–2 | | | 'about 12'. |
| | | | | Her. s. 1576 | | | |
| | | | | Ox. 1938 1082 | | | |

*Zapher Papoura, Chamber Tomb 56*

> *AE/NB* (N.D.v3); *DM/DB* 1904.
> *PreT* I.67.

| Ref. no. | Sketch | Description | Drawing | Sealing | Other examples | AE Cat. | Comments and plate reference |
|----------|--------|-------------|---------|---------|----------------|---------|------------------------------|
| V2 | | * | | Her. s. 416 | | | For differing views on its identification, see Section 3, the comment on N8. PLATE 5. |

## CONCORDANCE A

Col. 1    Museum Catalogue number.
    \* = nodules without seal impressions.
    # = missing nodules (of which sometimes plaster casts exist).
Col. 2 References to other examples of the same design. On the first occasion all examples are
    listed, after that there is only a cross-reference to the first.
Col. 3 Correlation with the tables at the end of each section above.

### HERAKLION: ARCHAEOLOGICAL MUSEUM

| | | | | | | |
|---|---|---|---|---|---|---|
| 106 | | O3 | | 147 | 1317 | |
| 107 | | G2 | | 148 | | R2 |
| 108 | | O4 | | 149 | | S4 |
| 109 | | J2 | | 150 | | S6 |
| 110 | | N2 | | 151 | | T2 |
| 111 | | N6 | | 152 | | S5 |
| 112 | | N11 | | 153 } | | |
| 113 | | G11 | | 154 } | | R102 |
| 114 } | 168/1 } | K2 } | | 155 | | R89 |
| 115 } | 168/2 } | K11 } | | 156 | 224 | O7 |
| 116 | | O11 | | 157 | | R91 |
| 117* | | N12 | | 158 | 662 | R32 |
| 118 | | O5 | | 159 | | Td |
| 119 | 401 | Vc | | 160 } | | Q19 |
| | 403 | | | 161 } | | |
| 120 | 199 | | | 162 | | Q13 |
| 121 | | N10 | | 163 | | R92 |
| 122 | | N7 | | 164 | | K3 |
| 123 | | F1 | | 165 | | G12 |
| 124 | | N13 | | 166/1–3 | 141 | M1–5 |
| 125* | | J4 | | 167 | | K8 |
| 126 | Ox. 1938. 982 | Pa | | 168/1 } | 114 | K2 } |
| 127 | | | | /2 } | | K11 } |
| 128 | | Pb | | /3 | 141 | M1–5 |
| 129 | Ox. 1938. 1016 | J1 | | /4 | | |
| | Ox. 1938. 1152 | | | /5 | | L? |
| | 1628 | | | /6 | | L? |
| 130 | | H? | | /7* | | |
| 131 | | Pe | | /8* | | |
| 132 | | P73 | | 169*# | (=Ox. 1910. 206) | P76 |
| 133 | | O2 | | 170 | | H2 |
| 134 } | | Q14 | | 171 | | P68 |
| 135 } | | | | 172 | | H1 |
| 136 | | G8 | | 173 | | P52 |
| 137 | | G7 | | 174 | | P54 |
| 138 | | | | 175# | (=Ox. 1910. 207) | P75 |
| 139/1–2 | | O12 | | 176 | | H4 |
| 140 | | Pc | | 177 | | P57 |
| 141/1–2 | 166/1–3 | M1–5 | | 178 | | P74 |
| | 168/3 | | | 179 | | P71 |
| 142 | | | | 180 | | Pf |
| 143 | | Q20 | | 181 | | P59 |
| 144 | | Pd | | 182 | | P60 |
| 145 | 247 | | | 183* | | P77 |
| | 1020 | | | 184 | | P55 |
| | 1280 | | | 185 | 195 | P67 |
| 146 | | J3 | | 186* | | H? |
| 147 | 313 | | | 187* | | P78 |

| | | |
|---|---|---|
| 188 | | |
| 189 | | P70 |
| 190 | | P72 |
| 191 | | P50 |
| 192 | | P69 |
| 193* | | G17 |
| 194 | | P58 |
| 195 | 185 | P66 |
| 196 | | H? |
| 197 | | H? |
| 198 | | P61 |
| 199 | 120 | |
| 200 | | P56 |
| 201 | | |
| 202 | | H? |
| 203 | | H? |
| 204* | | |
| 205 | | O1 |
| 206 | | P63 |
| 207 | | P65 |
| 208 | | R7 |
| 209 | | G10 } |
| | 376/1–2 | G9 } |
| | Mus. Goul. 807 | |
| 210/1a–b,2 | | R29 } |
| | 228 | R25 } |
| | 231 | R17 } |
| 211 | | R13 |
| 212 } | 1000 | R6 |
| 213 } | 1005 | |
| | 1597 | |
| 214 } | 258/1 | K4 |
| 215 } | 1296 | K12 |
| | Ox. 1938. 1014a-d | Q21 |
| | Ox. n. No. 7 | R53 |
| | 299 | K7 |
| | 258/2 | F2 |
| 216 | | R86 |
| 217 | | |
| 218 | | R44 |
| 219 } | 252 | R43 |
| 220 } | | |
| 221 | | R10 |
| 222 | | R15 |
| 223 | | |
| 224 | 156 | O7 |
| 225 | | O6 |
| 226 } | | R103 |
| 227 } | | |
| 228 | 210 | R25 |
| 229 | | R36 |
| 231 | 210 | R17 |
| 232 | | cf. R17 |
| 233 } | | |
| 234 } | | |
| 235 } | 256/1–12 | R88 |
| 236 | 1346 | |
| 237 } | | |
| 238 } | | |

| | | |
|---|---|---|
| 239 | 241 | G5 } |
| | Ox. 1938. 1080 | G6 } |
| 240 | 1023 | G3 |
| | 1542 | |
| 241 | 239 | G5 |
| 242 } | 268 | R50 |
| 243 } | 274 | |
| 244 } | 1557 | |
| 245 } | 1558 | |
| 246 | | |
| 247 | 145 | |
| 248 | | |
| 249 | | H |
| 250 | | R8 |
| 251 | | R9 |
| 252 | 219 | R43 |
| 253 | | N1 |
| 254 | | |
| 255 | 1529 | |
| 256/1–12 | 233 | R88 |
| /13 | 257/1–5 | R81 |
| | 261–2 | |
| | 269 | |
| | 273 | |
| | 275/1–6 | |
| | 1365 | |
| | 1380 | |
| | Ox. 1938. 1046 | |
| /14 | | |
| /15 | | |
| /16 | | |
| 257/1–5 | 256/13 | R81 |
| 258/1 | 214 | K12 } |
| /2 | | F2 } |
| 259 | | C15 |
| 260 | 361 | R60 } |
| | 271 | R63 } |
| 261 } | 256/13 | R81 |
| 262 } | | |
| 263 | | |
| 264 | | R100 |
| 265 | 275/7 | R18 |
| | 365–6 | |
| 266 | | R22 |
| 267 | | R61 |
| 268 | 242 | R50 |
| 269 | 256/13 | R81 |
| 270 | | R34 |
| 271 | 260 | R63 |
| 272 | | R66 |
| 273 | 256/13 | R81 |
| 274 | 242 | R50 |
| 275/1–6 | 256/13 | R81 |
| /7 | 265 | R18 |
| /8 | | |
| 276 | | |

| | | |
|---|---|---|
| 277 } | Ox. 1938. 1015a–b | R1 } |
| 278 } | SMa | R51 } |
| 279 } | | R54 } |
| 280 } | | |
| 281 } | | |
| 282 } | | |
| 283 | | Q22 |
| 284 | | G13 |
| 285 | | G14 |
| 286 | | |
| 287 | | R69 |
| 288 | | R85 |
| 289 | | R3 |
| 290 | | |
| 291 | | R35 |
| 292/1–4 | 294 } 1234 } | R19 } R30 } |
| 293 | | R4 |
| 294 | 292 | R19 |
| 295 | | K6 } R46 } |
| | 329 } 1208 } | |
| 296 | | K10 |
| 297 | | K5 |
| 298 | | K9 |
| 299 | 214 | K7 |
| 300 } 301 } | | R27 } |
| | 305/1–2 } 306–7 } | R12 } |
| | 314 } 323–4 } 1237 } 1625 } | R14 } |
| 302 | | R33 |
| 303 | | R23 |
| 304 | | R21 |
| 305/1–2 } 306 } 307 } | 300 | R12 |
| 308/1–3 | 1257 1398 1518 311/6 | R74 } R97 } |
| 309/1–5 | | R83 |
| /6–7 | | R59 |
| /8 | | R82 |
| 310 | | R42 |
| 311/1–5 | | R84 |
| | 330/5–7, 10 | |
| /6 | 308 | R97 |
| /7 | 1229 | R71 |
| 312 | | |
| 313 | 147 | |
| 314 | 300 | R14 |
| 315 | | R41 |
| 316 } 317 } 318 } | | R49 |

| | | |
|---|---|---|
| 319 | | R77 |
| 320/1 | | R79 |
| /2 | 406 | Ta |
| 321 | | R37 |
| 322 | | |
| 323 } 324 } | 300 | R14 |
| 325/1–2 } 326/1 } | | |
| /2 } 327 } | 1548 | |
| 328 | 1008 | |
| | 1223 | |
| | 1282 | |
| 329 | 295 | R46 |
| 330/1–4 | 1247 1614 | R52 |
| /5–7, 10 | 311/1–2 | R84 |
| /8–9 | | R48 |
| 331 } 332 } | 1604 | R76 |
| 333/1–6 } 334/1–2 } 335/1–4 } | 387/1–2 1426 1449 | L13, 25–6 |
| | Ox. 1938. 1439a–c | |
| 336 | | L50 |
| 337 } 338 } 339 } | 350–2 | L49 |
| 340 | | L43 |
| 341 | | |
| 342 | 413 | L18–9 |
| 343 | | L47 |
| 344 | | La |
| 345 | 399 | L8–12, 27, 45 |
| 346 | | L16–7? |
| 347 | | L? |
| 348 | | L42 |
| 349 | 398 | L31–3? |
| 350 } 351 } 352 } | 337 | L49 |
| 353 | 660/1–2 | |
| 354 | | L16–7? |
| 355 { a ... b | 356/1a 356/2 1248 356/1b } | L? |
| 356/1 { a b | 355a 355b | |
| /2 | 355a | |
| 357 | | L? |
| 358 | | L36 |
| 359 | | L? |
| 360 | | Q16 |
| 361 | 260 | R60 |
| 362 | | K16 |
| 363 | | Tf |
| 364 | | R16 |

| | | |
|---|---|---|
| 365 } 366 } | 265 | $R_{18}$ |
| 367 | | $R_{38}$ |
| 368 | | |
| 369 | 1275 | Ec |
| 370 | 381 | |
| 371 | | |
| 372 | | |
| 373 | | |
| 374 | | $L_{1-6}$ |
| 375 | | Vb |
| 376/1–2 | 209 | $G_9$ |
| 377/1–3 | Ox. 1938. 1068 | Va |
| 378 | | |
| 379 | | |
| 380 | | |
| 381 | 370 | |
| 382 | | Ca |
| 383/1–9 | 395 | $L_{46}$ |
| 384/1–2 | | $L_{15, 22}$ |
| 385 | | $L_{20}$ |
| 386 | | $L_{24}$ |
| 387/1–2 | 333 | $L_{13, 25}$ |
| 388/1–9 | Ox. 1938, 1440a–b | $L_{7, 40}$ |
| 389 | | L? |
| 390a | | $L_{1-6}$ |
| 390b | | $L_{1-6}$ |
| 391 | | $L_{38}$ |
| 392 | | Cc |
| 393 | | $L_{39}$ |
| 394 | | $L_{35}$ |
| 395 | 383 | $L_{46}$ |
| 396 | | $L_{48}$ |
| 397 | | Lb |
| 398 | 349 | $L_{31-3}$? |
| 399 | 345 | $L_{8-12, 27}$ |
| 400/1–3 | 402? 1024 1600 | Vd |
| 401 | 119 | Vc |
| 402# | 400? | Vd |
| 403 | 119 | Vc |
| 404 | | $L_{41}$ |
| 405 | | $L_{8-12}$? |
| 406 | 320 | Ta |
| 407 | 411–2 1200 | T? |
| 408 | | T? |
| 409 | | T? |
| 410# | | |
| 411 } 412 } | 407 | T? |
| 413 | 342 | $L_{18-9}$ |
| 415/1–2 | 1576–9 Ox. 1938. 1082 | $V_1$ |
| 416 | | $V_2$ |
| 417 | 1269 | $U_{112}$ |
| 418 | | $E_1$ |

| | | |
|---|---|---|
| 419 | | $U_{107}$ |
| 421 | | $U_2$ |
| 422 | | $U_{19}$ |
| 423 | | $U_{12}$ |
| 424 | | $U_7$ |
| 425 | | $T_1$ |
| 426/1–3 | | Tc |
| 650 | | U? |
| 651 | | $U_{31}$ |
| 652 | | $U_{104}$ |
| 653 | | U? |
| 654 | | $U_{106}$ |
| 655 | | U? |
| 656 | | $U_{115}$ |
| 657 | | $U_{105}$ |
| 658 | | $U_{66}$ |
| 659 | | $U_{117}$ |
| 660/1–2 | 353 | |
| 661 | | Cb |
| 662 | 158 | $R_{32}$ |
| 663 | | $U_{114}$? |
| 664/1–2 | | $C_{11}$ |
| 665 | | $R_{101}$ |
| 666 | | Ve |
| 667 | | $C_{60}$ |
| 668 | | $C_{10}$ |
| 669 | | $C_9$ |
| 670 | | $C_{43}$ |
| 671/1–4 | Ox. n. No. 8 | Ce |
| 997 | | |
| 998 | | |
| 999 | | |
| 1000 | 212 | $R_6$ |
| 1001 | | |
| 1002 | | |
| 1003 | | |
| 1004 | 1015 | |
| 1005 | 212 | $R_6$ |
| 1006 | | |
| 1007 | | |
| 1008 | 328 | |
| 1009 | | |
| 1010 | 1551 | |
| 1011 | | |
| 1012 | | |
| 1013 | | |
| 1014 | | |
| 1015 | 1004 | |
| 1016 | | |
| 1017 | | |
| 1018 | | |
| 1019 | | |
| 1020 | 145 | |
| 1021 | | |
| 1022 | | |
| 1023 | 240 | $G_3$ |
| 1024 | 400 | Vd |

| | | |
|---|---|---|
| 1025 | | |
| 1026 | | |
| 1027 | | |
| 1028 | | |
| 1029 | | R39 |
| 1030 | | |
| 1031 | | |
| 1032 | | |
| 1033 | | |
| 1034 | | |
| 1035 | 1271 | |
| 1036 | | |
| 1037 | | |
| 1038 | 1311 | |
| | 1362 | |
| 1039 | | |
| 1040 | | |
| 1041 | | |
| 1042 | | |
| 1043 | | |
| 1044 | 1206/1–2 | R45 |
| | 1608 | |
| 1045 | | |
| 1046 | 1030 | |
| 1047 | | |
| 1048 | | |
| 1180 | | |
| 1181 | | |
| 1182/1–2 | | |
| 1183 | | R106 |
| 1184 | | |
| 1185 | | |
| 1186 | | |
| 1187 | | |
| 1188 | | R36 |
| 1189 | | R105 |
| 1190 | | |
| 1191 | | |
| 1192 | | |
| 1193 | | |
| 1194 | | |
| 1195 | | |
| 1196 | | |
| 1197/1–2 | | R67 |
| 1198 | | |
| 1199 | | |
| 1200 | 407 | T? |
| 1201 | | |
| 1202 | | |
| 1203 | | Q9 |
| 1204/1–3 | 1640 | Q2–3 |
| | 1677 | |
| | 1678 | |
| | 1679 | |
| 1205 | | |
| 1206/1–2 | 1044 | R45 |
| 1207 | 1217 | Q7 |
| 1208 | 295 | R46 |

| | | |
|---|---|---|
| 1209 | 1228 | Q15 |
| | Ox. 1938. 1047 | Q17 |
| 1210 | 1361 | R68 |
| | 1602 | |
| | 1606 | |
| | 1610 | |
| 1211 | | |
| 1212 | | |
| 1213 | | |
| 1214 | | R20 |
| 1215 | | L8–12 |
| 1216 | | |
| 1217 | 1207 | Q7 |
| 1218 | | |
| 1219 | | K13 |
| 1220 | | |
| 1221 | | L? |
| 1222 | | Q4 |
| 1223 | 328 | |
| 1224 | | |
| 1225 | | |
| 1226/1–2 | | Q6 |
| 1227 | | · R11 |
| 1228 | 1209 | Q11? |
| 1229 | 311/7 | R71 |
| 1230 | | Q1(?) |
| 1231 | 1250 | |
| 1232 | | |
| 1233 | | |
| 1234 | 292 | R19 |
| 1235 | | R28 |
| 1236 | | |
| 1237 | 300 | R14 |
| 1238 | | R70 |
| 1239 | | |
| 1240 | | L29 |
| 1241 | 1288 | |
| 1242 | | |
| 1243 | | |
| 1244 | | |
| 1245 | | |
| 1246 | | Q8 |
| 1247 | 330/1–4 | R52 |
| 1248 | 355a | L? |
| 1249 | | |
| 1250 | 1231 | |
| 1251 | | |
| 1252 | 1352 | L? |
| 1253 | | |
| 1254 | | |
| 1255 | | |
| 1256 | | |
| 1257 | 308 | R74 |
| 1258 | | Q13 |
| 1259 | | L14 |
| 1260 | | L? |
| 1261 | | |
| 1262 | | |

| | | | | | |
|---|---|---|---|---|---|
| 1263 | | | 1278 | |
| 1264 | | L1–6? | 1279 | |
| 1265 | | | 1280 | 145 |
| 1266 | | | 1281 | |
| 1267 | | | 1282 | 328 |
| 1268 | | | 1283 | |
| 1269 | 417 | | 1284 | |
| 1270 | | | 1285 | |
| 1271 | 1035 | | 1286 | |
| 1272 | | | 1287 | |
| 1273 | | | 1288 | 1241 |
| 1274 | | | 1289 | |
| 1275 | 369 | | 1290 | |
| 1276 | | | 1291 | |
| 1277 | | | 1292 | |

## Addendum

A further 350 or so sealings from Evans's Knossos excavations have turned up since the original publication of my article (Her. s. 1294–1652, 1677–1682, 1691). Only those with an identifiable provenance or repeat impression are listed below.

| | | | | | | |
|---|---|---|---|---|---|---|
| 1296 | 214 | | 1398 | 308 | R74 |
| 1301 | 1330, 1337, 1343, 1344, | | 1408 | 1490 | cf. R59 |
| | 1347, 1353, 1356, 1359, | | | 1508 | |
| | 1376, 1383, 1388, 1390, | | | 1526/1–2 | |
| | 1392, 1393, 1395, 1399, | | 1426 | 334 | |
| | 1402, 1405, 1406, 1411, | | 1449 | 334 | |
| | 1412, 1414, 1416, 1417, | | 1490 ⎫ | 1408 | cf. R59 |
| | 1418, 1422, 1427, 1430, | | 1508 ⎭ | | |
| | 1431, 1432, 1433, 1434, | | 1518 | 308 | R74 |
| | 1439, 1440, 1441, 1442, | | 1526/1–2 | 1408 | cf. R59 |
| | 1444, 1450, 1454, 1463, | | 1529 | 255 | |
| | 1465, 1471, 1472, 1485, | | 1542 | 240 | G3–4 |
| | 1492, 1498, 1499, 1501, | | 1548 | 327 | |
| | 1503, 1509, 1510, 1515, | | 1551 | 1010 | |
| | 1516, 1599 | | 1557 ⎫ | 242 | R50 |
| 1302 | 1373 | R57? | 1558 ⎭ | | |
| 1303 | | Q18 | 1576 ⎫ | 415 | V1 |
| 1305 | 1306 | | 1577 ⎪ | | |
| 1311 | 1038 | | 1578 ⎪ | | |
| 1317 | 147 | | 1579 ⎭ | | |
| 1320 | 1424 | | 1597 | 212 | R6 |
| | 1469 | | 1600 | 400 | Vd |
| 1339 | 1375 | | 1602 | 1210 | R68 |
| | 1445 | | 1603 | | R75 |
| 1341 | 1369, 1396, 1401, 1415, | | 1604 | 331 | R76 |
| | 1419, 1420 | | 1605 | | R80 |
| 1345 | 1363, 1381, 1391, 1410, | | 1606 | 1210 | R68 |
| | 1486 | | 1608 | 1044 | R45 |
| 1346 | 233 | R88 | 1609 | | R73 |
| 1352 | 1252 | L? | 1610 | 1210 | R68 |
| 1354 | 1436 | | 1614 | 330 | R52 |
| | 1480 | | 1617 | | R87 |
| 1361 | 1210 | R68 | | | |
| 1362 | 1038 | | 1620 | | L? |
| 1365 ⎫ | 256/13 | R81 | 1625 | 300 | R12 |
| 1380 ⎭ | | | 1626 | | L? |
| 1387 | 1484 | | 1628 | 129 | J1 |

| | | | | | |
|---|---|---|---|---|---|
| 1634 | | K15? | 1677 ⎫ | 1204 | Q2-3 |
| 1639 | | Q12 | 1678 ⎬ | | |
| 1640 | 1204 | Q2-3 | 1679 ⎭ | | |
| 1643 | | R24? | 1691 | | R107 |
| 1646 | | R31 | | | |

## OXFORD: ASHMOLEAN MUSEUM

| | | | | | | |
|---|---|---|---|---|---|---|
| AE 1199zeta | Her. s. 383 | L46 | 1938. 1068 | Her. s. 377 | Va |
| AE 1199u | | | 1938. 1080 | Her. s. 239 | G6 |
| 1910. 206* | (=Her. s. 169) | | 1938. 1082 | Her. s. 415 | V1 |
| 1910. 207 | (=Her. s. 175) | | 1938. 1152 | Her. s. 129 | J1 |
| 1938.858* | | | 1938. 1153a | | |
| 1938. 861 | | G15 | 1938. 1153b | | |
| 1938. 939 | | Te | 1938. 1439a–c | Her. s. 333 | L13, 25 |
| 1938. 940 | | H3 | 1938. 1440a–b | Her. s. 388 | L7, 40 |
| 1938. 941 | | | 1938. 1441 (Knossos?) | | |
| 1938. 947a–b | | R94 | 1941. 180* | | R |
| 1938. 948 | | | Ox. n. No. 1 (1988. 45) | | |
| 1938. 981 | | K1 | No. 2 (1988. 43) | | |
| 1938. 982 | Her. s. 126 | Pa | No. 3 (AE 1799) | | L? |
| 1938. 1014a–d | Her. s. 214 | K4, Q21 | No. 4 (1988. ) | | |
| 1938. 1015a–b | Her. s. 277 | R54 | No. 5 (1988. 55) | | |
| 1938. 1016 | Her. s. 129 | J1 | No. 6 (1988. 59) | | |
| 1938. 1046 | Her. s. 256e | R81 | No. 7 | Her. s. 214 | K4 |
| 1938. 1047 | Her. s. 1209 | Q17 | No. 8 | Her. s. 671 | Ce |

# CONCORDANCE B

Col. 1    Heraklion Museum Catalogue number or reference as it appeared in *BSA* 60 (1965), and where it differs from the new Museum inventory number.

Col. 2    New Heraklion Museum Inventory number.

| | | | |
|---|---|---|---|
| 139i–ii | 139/1–2 | 275c | 275/7 |
| 141i–ii | 141/1–2 | 292i | 292/1 |
| 166i | 166/2 | 292ii | 292/3 |
| 166ii | 166/1 | (292iii) | 292/2 |
| 166iii | 166/3 | (292iv) | 292/4 |
| 168ai | 168/1 | 305i–ii | 305/1–2 |
| 168aii | 168/2 | 308i–iii | 308/1–3 |
| 168b | 168/3 | 309ai–v | 309/1–5 |
| 168c | 168/6 | 309b | 309/8 |
| 168d | 168/5 | 309ci–ii | 309/6–7 |
| 168e | 168/4 | 311ai–ii | 311/1–2 |
| 168f | 168/7 | 311aiii–iv | 311/4–5 |
| 168g | 168/8 | 311av | 311/3 |
| 210i | 210/2 | 311b | 311/6 |
| 210ii | 210/1b | 311/c | 311/7 |
| 230 | 210/1a | 320a | 320/2 |
| 256ai–xii | 256/1–12 | 320b | 320/1 |
| 256b | 256/14 | 325 | 325/1 |
| 256c | 256/15 | 326i–ii | 326/1–2 |
| 256d | 256/16 | 330ai–iii | 330/5–7 |
| 256e | 256/13 | 330aiv | 330/10 |
| 257i–v | 257/1–5 | 330b | 330/8 |
| 258 (258i) | 258/1 | 330ci–iv | 330/1–4 |
| (258ii) | 258/2 | 333i–vi | 333/1–6 |
| 275ai–vi (viii) | 275/1–6 | 333vii | 335/3 |
| 275b | 275/8 | 334i–ii | 334/1–2 |

| | | | |
|---|---|---|---|
| 335i–ii | 335/1–2 | 39 | 1213 |
| 335iii | 335/4 | 40 | 1214 |
| 356 | 356/1 | 41 | 1206/2 |
| 376 | 376/1 | 42 | 400/1 |
| 377i | 377/1 | 43 | 1215 |
| 377ii | 377/3 | 44 | 1216 |
| 383i–ix | 383/1–9 | 45 | 1217 |
| 384i–ii | 384/1–2 | 46 | 377/2 |
| 387i–ii | 387/1–2 | 47 | 1218 |
| 388i–ix | 388/1–9 | 48 | 1219 |
| 390a | 390/1 | 49 | 1220 |
| 390b | 390/2 | 50 | 1221 |
| 400 | 400/3 | 51 | 1222 |
| 415i–ii | 415/1–2 | 52 | 1223 |
| 426i–iii | 426/1–3 | 53 | 1224 |
| 660i–ii | 660/1–2 | 54 | 1225 |
| 664i–ii | 664/1–2 | 55 | 1226/2 |
| 671i–iv | 671/1–4 | 56 | 1227 |
| 1034 | 1035 | 57 | 1226/1 |
| 1035 | 1034 | 58 | 1234 |
| n. No. 1 | 1180 | 59 | 1228 |
| 2 | 1181 | 60 | 1230 |
| 3 | 1182/1 | 61 | 1231 |
| 4 | 1183 | 62 | 1232 |
| 5 | 1184 | 63 | 1233 |
| 6 | 1185 | 64 | 1235 |
| 7 | 292/2 | 65 | 1236 |
| 8 | 1186 | 66 | 1237 |
| 9 | 1187 | 67 | 1238 |
| 10 | 1188 | 68 | 1239 |
| 11 | 1189 | 69 | 1240 |
| 12 | 1190 | 70 | 1241 |
| 13 | 1191 | 71 | 356/2 |
| 14 | 1192 | 72 | 1247 |
| 15 | 1193 | 73 | 330/9 |
| 16 | 1194 | 74 | 1242 |
| 17 | 1195 | 75 | 1243 |
| 18 | 1196 | 76 | 1244 |
| 19i–ii | 1197/1–2 | 77 | 1245 |
| 20 | 1198 | 78 | 1246 |
| 21 | 1211 | 79 | 1204/2 |
| 22 | 1199 | 80 | 325/2 |
| 23 | 1200 | 81 | 1249 |
| 24 | 1201 | 82 | 1248 |
| 25 | 1182/2 | 83 | 1250 |
| 26 | 1202 | 84 | 1251 |
| 27 | 1203 | 85 | 1255 |
| 28 | 311/3 | 86 | 1252 |
| 29 | 1204/1 | 87 | 1253 |
| 30 | 1205 | 88 | 1254 |
| 31 | 1206/1 | 89 | 1259 |
| 32 | 1207 | 90 | 1258 |
| 33 | 1208 | 91 | 1256 |
| 34 | 1204/3 | 92 | — |
| 35 | 1209 | 93 | 1257 |
| 36 | 1210 | 94 | 1229 |
| 37 | 292/4 | 95 | 258/2 |
| 38 | 1212 | 96 | — |

| | | | |
|---|---|---|---|
| 97 | 376/2 | 117 | 1276 |
| 98 | — | 118 | 1277 |
| 99 | — | 119 | 1278 |
| 100 | 1260 | 120 | 1287 |
| 101 | 1261 | 121 | 1280 |
| 102 | 400/2 | 122 | 1281 |
| 103 | 1262 | 123 | 1282 |
| 104 | 1263 | 124 | 1283 |
| 105 | 1264 | 125 | 1284 |
| 106 | 1265 | 126 | 1285 |
| 107 | 1266 | 127 | 1279 |
| 108 | 1267 | 128 | 1289 |
| 109 | 1268 | 129 | 1291 |
| 110 | 1269 | 130 | 1293 |
| 111 | 1270 | 131 | 1286 |
| 112 | 1271 | 132 | 1288 |
| 113 | 1272 | 133 | 1290 |
| 114 | 1273 | 134 | 1292 |
| 115 | 1274 | 135 | — |
| 116 | 1275 | | |

# APPENDIX A

*Linear B: inscriptions incised on sealings*

| Sealing | Ref. no. | SM ii. 64–65, 89. | Inscription Class. Nos. |
|---|---|---|---|
| Her. s. 108 | O4 | 1701 (Za 31) | Ws 1701 |
| 117 | N12 | | |
| 118 | O5 | 1702 (Za 01) | Ws 1702 |
| 119 | Vc | | |
| 121 | N10 | | |
| 122 | N7 | | |
| 124 | N13 | | |
| 125 | J4 | 1707 (Za 51) | Ws 1707 |
| 129 | J1 | | |
| 138 | — | | |
| 156 | O7 | | |
| 193 | G7 | | |
| 224 | O7 | | |
| 225 | O6 | | |
| 258/2 | F2 | | |
| 401 } 403 } | Vc { | 1704 (Za 02) 1705 (Za 21) | Ws 1704 Ws 1705 |
| — | R104 | 1713 | |
| — | C45 | | |
| — | S1 | 1708 (Za 61) 1636 | Ws 1708 |
| — | U93 (?) | | |
| Ox. 1938.858 | — | | Wb 8207 |
| Ox. 1938.861 | G15 { | 1709 (Za 71) 1706 (Za 41) | Ws 8152 Ws 1706 |
| 1938.1080 | G6 | 1703 (Za 11) | Ws 1703 |
| 1938.1152 | J1 | | Ws 8153 |
| 1941.180 | R { | 1714c 1653 1712 | Wb 1817 |
| — | R { | 1714a–b 1712 | Wb 1816 |

1714 (1712) a–c, found in the same area as R53, are described by Evans *(AE/NB* 1902.48) as a 'new kind of round tablet'. Although they bear no impressions, the shape of the perforated nodules classes them among the sealings. In absence of the original, it is uncertain whether the sign on U93 is a countermark or part of the seal design.

## APPENDIX B

*Seal-types common to several deposits*

Interrelation between deposits of sealings in various parts of the palace is more apparent than actual. There are six certain cases:

1. Standing bitch: F2, K4, K7, K12, Q21, R53.
2. Man standing before seated goddess: K2, K11 (but probably not C2).
3. Seated goddess and two attendants: Q22 (clay matrix), R1, R51, R54.
4. Kneeling bull: K6, R46.
5. Contorted lion: S1, Vc.
6. Man and bull: G5, G6.

Other possible correspondences are Q17 with D21, and G3 with Her. s. 1023 which may have come from Magazine 8, as discussed above. Her. s. 1269 from the Main Palace was possibly impressed by the same seal as U112. There may have been sealings in the Rooms of the Egyptian Beans and of the Clay Signet similar to those in the Room of the Seal Impressions as Evans records (*BSA* 7 (1900–1) 16), but they are not described in the Notebooks nor can any be identified in the surviving material. Several of the types thought to be common to different deposits turn out to be single sealings. There is always the possibility that other copies were found and have since been mislaid, but on the whole allocation of these types to various places is the result of duplicate description and misattribution (e.g. R88 (E8), Ca (A5), K2 (C2), E3 (D3). Q8 (A7) has been said to be similar to Vc/d and G8 to U106 but in both cases different seals were involved, and G8 bears neither stylistic nor pictorial resemblance to U106.

A type with fighting warriors (Her. s. 369, Her. s. 1275), Plate 32(b), is identical with some sealings from Hagia Triada (Her. s. 526i–iii, 595, 596; cf. D. Levi 'Le Cretule di H. Triada' *ASAtene* 8–9 (1925–6) 123, fig. 130, 144, fig. 160).

# Section 3

# Some observations and notes on the sealings, their illustrations and recording

M.R. POPHAM

The comments and notes given below have arisen for the most part from aspects of the sealings, their photographs, drawings and Evans's Notebooks which have attracted the author's interest during the preparation of this work. The bibliography cited does not pretend in any way to be complete, nor the very occasional references to comparisons which, it is hoped, will now be completed by scholars familiar with all the material and especially the seals. The few instances are mentioned when the author (M.R.P.) and Margaret Gill (M.A.V.G.) have differing views on identifications and other matters, giving the grounds for their varying opinions.

The abbreviations Betts, Kenna and Younger used in both this section and on the captions to the PLATES are included in the list in the Preliminaries.

The shapes and types of nodules of the latest sealings are listed according to her typology by J. Weingarten in 'The sealing structures of Minoan Crete, Part II' in *Oxford Journal of Archaeology* 7 (1988) 20–5, which could be valuably expanded by a fuller description of the impressions on the backs of sealings and, where applicable, the size of the thread or string around which they were fashioned.

Evans's discussions of individual sealings and their motives, which remain fundamental, are scattered throughout the four volumes of *PM* though largely concentrated in *PM* IV.591–618, where the larger of the deposits are also listed. References to these discussions, not given here, are to be found in the Index Volume or may be found by consulting the passages where they are illustrated, given in the captions to PLATES 27–32.

G3      For a composite drawing of Her. s. 240 + 1023 by M.A.V.G. see PLATE 32(a). Evans's Handlist of tablets for 1900 mentions only two sealings (*OKT* p.34), presumably omitting G1 as clearly earlier and out of context. His descriptions there correspond with those of his NB entry for G3 and G5. This must shed some doubt as to whether Her. s. 1023, though from the same seal as G3, was in fact found in Magazine 4. See M.A.V.G.'s comments in Section 2. Younger, '1410–1385 BC'.

G6      Countermarked and endorsed, PLATE 33 and Gill, fig. 3, 11. Kenna, p.46, 'LM II'.

G8      Evans's misinterpretation of G8, 'corn' (on PLATE 33), noted by M.A.V.G. persisted into *PM* IV.626 and fig. 613 as 'barley corn'. Dated Kenna, p.44, 'LM II'.

G9–10    A photographic reconstruction at PLATE 25 from both examples. Kenna, p.44 no. 43, 'LH II', a Mainland attribution, wrongly located in the Little Palace.

G12      Dated Younger, '1550–1500'.

G15      Countermarked and endorsed, PLATE 34 and Gill, fig. 3, 10. Dated with a Mainland attribution by Kenna, p.44, Part III,1, 'LH II'.

J1       Both examples countermarked and endorsed but differently in each case, Gill, fig. 2, 8 and fig. 3, 12. Two drawings exist of Her. s. 129, not reproduced here, *BSA* 60 (1965) plate 5 (Evans, not published) and Kenna, fig. 3 and dated p.48, 'LM IIIA'. See also Kenna, *Cretan Seals* 45S illustrated plate 17.

J2       Complete design reconstructed by M.A.V.G., PLATE 32(c), repeated from CMS *Die Kretisch-Mykenische Glyptik und ihre gegenwärtigen Probleme* (1974) where she discusses the sealing and comments on the vertical and horizontal fractures and repair apparent on the impression, p.32. Dated Younger, '1550–1500', and Kenna, p.44 no. 2, 'LM II'.

J3       Dated Kenna, p.44 no. 3, 'LM II'.

J4       Nodule without impression but inscribed on all three sides, Gill, fig. 4, 19 and *OKT* plate XVI(a) which also reproduces the passage containing the description of J5 'hind part of bull' not included here.

J5       See above. Several fragmentary sealings without provenance would suit, the claim of Her. s. 145 (PLATE 19) being merely its early inventory number just before J3, Her. s. 146.

K2       The cross-hatching on the dress of the drawing on PLATE 27 from *PM* is not obvious on the impressions. It may derive from Evans's sketch at PLATE 35 which had been cut out for redrawing.

K4 and   K4 has been grouped on PLATE 4 with K12 and Q21 since M.R.P. can see no
K12      definite way of distinguishing them from Evans' sketches and remarks. The lack of teats on his sketch of K4, though present on that of K7 (and called a bitch), might suggest a poor impression, i.e. Her. s. 215, but see M.A.V.G.'s comments in Section 2.

K5       Dated Younger, 'mid to late 14th century'.

K6       Evans seems not to have recognized, when sketching R46, that it was a duplicate of this sealing found earlier the same year, though noting in both instances that they had been impressed, unusually, by an amygdaloid (PLATES 35 and 43). Dated Younger, '1500–1475'.

K9       Dated Younger, 'early 14th century'.

Ka       An addition at this late stage, *PM* IV.544, is highly dubious. I suspect that it is a misplaced note on K1 meant to be an example of the motive of lion attacking bull, discussed slightly earlier on pp. 534 f. Such a note could have derived from the publication of K1 in *PM* I.716 fig. 539(b) where it is grouped with other sealings given the general caption of 'Flying Gallop on MM III Seal-impressions'; the 'rocky background below' (p.717) is additional to his early description of it at PLATE 35. This might account, too, for the otherwise unjustified locating of the sealing (in *PM* IV) as having been found 'under stratigraphic conditions pointing to about the same date' which in its context means LM IB. Another example, I fear, of Evans adjusting the stratigraphy to suit the date of the signet, and overriding the evidence for the context of the sealing. For other apparently similar instances, see the comment on Q22, R8–9, R50 and R92.

K13      Dated Younger, '1410–1385'.

K16      Evans's sketch (PLATE 35) omits the two horizontal ?spears, as does *PM* I.694 fig. 516, repeated III 313 fig. 204. The more accurate drawing commissioned by Evans on PLATE 27 remained unpublished. The small fragment Q12 (PLATE 6) resembles it but has a different ground line. Dated Kenna, p.14 no. 4, 'LM II'.

M1–5      As Evans states in *BSA* 8 (1900–1) 28, the drawing at PLATE 27 is a composite one constructed from the various fragmentary sealings. A new drawing is overdue. There is faint evidence for the horns of consecration depicted on the roof of the building on Her. s. 166/2.

N1–13      As mentioned in Section 3 above, the sealings are discussed by J. Driessen in *An Early Destruction in the Mycenaean Palace at Knossos* (Leuven 1990) 63–66 and rather poorly illustrated on Illustr. 27 but with useful photographs of the reverses of N2, N6 and Her. s. 1546 (his s.o. 253). He cites the provisional dating of them given by I. Pini and J. Younger which is repeated in the entries below. New information is given that four sealings have recently been found with tablets which are said to be from the Room of the Chariot Tablets (fns. 219 and 233). One is a nodulus without impression; the other three are Her. s. 1546 (his s.o. 253), Her. s. 1547 (s.o. 254) and Her. s. 1548 (s.o. 255), illustrated here at PLATE 24. None would suit the unidentified N3, N4 and N5. There are two misreadings of Evans's handwriting; fn. 224 for 'shiny hollow' read 'string holes' and fn. 231 for 'topic' read 'device'.

N1      Kenna (1964), p.50 considers the 'rays' on the lion's body to be a re-engraving 'a Mainland alteration'. It is discussed and illustrated by I. Pini in *Philia Epi* 1, 302 and plate 52a in his study of Her. s. 255 + 1529 where both are linked with Near Eastern sun representations. The depiction of the muzzle is very similar to that on R18 (PLATE 25), while Kenna, *Cretan Seals* no. 315 = *PM* IV Suppl. plate LVj is a near 'look-alike'.

N2      Dated (see above) Pini, 'LM IIIA 1'; Younger, 'LM IIIA 1'.

N3      Her. s. 1375 (PLATE 23) is a possible candidate for 'uncertain device. bit of palm tree' (PLATE 36).

N4      Her. s. 1041 (PLATE 22) = Betts 31 would suit 'uncertain (eagle)' (PLATE 36). Evans's sketch of the string impressions should aid future identification.

N5      The shape, condition and early Inventory number suggest Her. s. 138 (PLATE 19) as a possibility but its poorly preserved impression cannot be matched with Evans's sketch and comment 'apparently woman and shrine' (PLATE 36).

N6      Cited for comparative purposes and illustrated in I.A. Papastolou, *Ta Sphragismata ton Hanion*, Athens 1977 (in Greek) plate 46st. Dated (see above) Pini, 'LM IIIA 1'; Younger, 'LM II-IIIA 1'.

N7      For the superscription see PLATE 37. Kenna, fig. 5, reproduced on PLATE 27, is not very accurate: cf. Gill, fig. 2, 2. Dated (see above) Pini, 'LM IIIA 1'; Younger, 'LM IIIA 1'.

N8      The bracket on PLATE 5 indicates a rare difference of opinion between M.R.P. and M.A.V.G. M.R.P. is convinced that Evans's sketch and description 'with its head turned back' suits admirably Her. s. 416. However, it entails a mistaken entry in the Inventory where it is recorded as coming from Knossos Tomb 1904. Only one sealing is recorded in the publication in *PreT.* 67 under Tomb 56, where it is described as 'a small fragment of an animal' an understatement for Her. s. 416. *DM/DB* records only 'clay sealing'; *AE/NB* 'seal impression'. The entry for Her. s. 414 as 'purchased' could be a similar error as it is surely from Evans's excavation. M.A.V.G. considers that the shape of the sealing does not coincide with that of the impression and sees no reason to doubt the correctness of the entry in the Inventory, pointing out that its position indicates that it was registered between 1904 and 1908 and comes immediately after the entry for Her. s. 415/1–2, the sealings from the Royal Tomb indicating that it did come from a tomb at Knossos, which from the records could only be Zafer Papoura T.56. See comment on V2 below.

N10 and   For their superscriptions see PLATES 27, 37 and Gill, fig. 2, 1. Dated respectively
N13       (see above) Pini, 'LM IB-IIIA 1 and LM II-IIIA 1'; Younger, 'LM IIIA 1 and LM
          IIIA 1'.

Na        This looks to be a likely, and not untypical, confusion by Evans with some note
          giving a general description of the chariot tablets found in the same room.

O1        A clay matrix with elongated stem or handle, drawn PLATE 37 with comment
          'apparently lion and bull'. Discussed by J. Betts, *Kadmos* 6 (1967) 22 and I. Pini
          in *Hommage à Henri Van Effenterre* 78–9 with plate XV. Dated Younger, '1430–1405'.

O3        A large roundel with impressions of the same seal around the indented edge
          (PLATE 24). Sketched with comment 'Palm stem' for the object on right edge of
          impression (PLATE 37). It might belong to the late MM IIIB/LM IA fill below
          the stairway (*PM* II.810–11).

O4        The drawing, J. Betts, *Kadmos* 6 (1967) 39 fig. 11b, is repeated here, PLATE 28, as
          being more accurate than *PM* IV.617 fig. 604a, which, however, gives the endorse-
          ment as well. He discusses the relationship of its impression with Her. s. 250 and
          other bull-leaping depictions, p.28. Gill, fig. 2, 6. Dated by Kenna, p.47, 'early
          LM II or LM IB'; Younger, 'late 16th century'.

O5        Dated Younger, '1410–1385'.

O6        Dated Younger, '1500–1475'.

O7        Both impressions are countermarked with the same sign. Gill, fig. 2, 5 and Kenna,
          p.45 fig. 4 = PLATE 28 and dated p.48, 'LM II'.

O11       A large roundel impressed by an early Minoan seal, illustrated at PLATE 24.

O12       Dated by Kenna, p.43, no. 51, 'LM II', repeating Evans's mislocation of it to the
          Archives Deposit (C51); Younger, '1410–1375'.

Q2–3      Impressions from the same signet; Younger, '1500–1485'.

Q5        Her. s. 1198 bracketed on PLATE 6 since M.R.P. has failed to persuade M.A.V.G.
          of the identification since the motive is a frequent one and she considers that the
          sealing and AE's sketch do not agree, especially in the depiction of the foliage.
          M.R.P., nevertheless, believes the description 'hindquarters of bull or cow'
          (PLATE 38), together with the shape drawn are sufficient to justify the identi-
          fication, though accepting that the sketch would then be shorthand. Moreover,
          Her. s. 1198 remained uncatalogued in 1965 as did Q1–4, and Q6–12.

Q7        Dated Younger, '1500–1475'.

Q8    'Bull? Rude or unfinished' with the comment '? were gems also engraved here ...', and in the margin 'cf. Armoury Deposit' (PLATE 39), possibly implying that Evans thought it might be an impression from the same signet as the Vc series.

Q11   'Hindquarters of a bull' would suit several unprovenanced sealings with the candidature of Her. s. 1393 (PLATE 23) being advanced only on the grounds that it was catalogued late, as were most of the Q series, and of its small size. M.A.V.G. prefers 1228 unfortunately not photographed.

Q12   See comment on K16 above.

Q13   The drawing on PLATE 28 repeated from *PM* IV.609 fig. 597B(e) is not very accurate.

Q14   Dated Younger, '1550–1500'.

Q15   Dated Younger, '1550–1500'.

Q17   Her. s. 1092 (PLATE 17), a duplicate found by N. Platon during his restoration work in the palace. No further details are known.

Q19   Humorously? Evans comments on the depiction as the Minotaur and Theseus in armour (PLATE 39). Theseus is omitted in the description *BSA* 7 (1900–1) 18 where fig. 7a is a different drawing from that at PLATE 28, without its couchant animal.

Q21   See K4 above and comments.

Q22   Though sketched (PLATE 40), no final drawing was made and published. The clay matrix and its relationship with the sealings R1, R51 and R54 has been the subject of considerable comment, e.g. Kenna, *Cretan Seals* 147, J. Betts, *Kadmos* 6 (1967) 21 and J. Weingarten in *Knossos, A Labyrinth of History* eds. D. Evely and others (1994) 186. Betts refutes Kenna's belief, following Evans, that the sealings were impressed by the matrix on the grounds of their clarity of outline. Betts suggests, p.27, that such replicas might have been 'for use by the ruler's representatives at other places within their dominion'. Weingarten with similar conclusions, places the signet owner within the Palace. As she observes, Evans's ascription of the matrix to a level not later than LM I in *PM* II.768, is not supported by *DM/DB*s or *AE/NB*s. Evans does record that it was found lower down than a large tablet in the upper earth (PLATE 40) and then goes on to describe fresco fragments from the same room, adding that it had two floor levels and that the frescoes were found below the first. He may have mistakenly conflated his two separate observations but, in any case, there is no known pottery evidence for the dating. The sealings in the Domestic Quarter with the same representation were, of course, in clear contexts belonging to the last destruction.

R2–99  The basic problems regarding Evans's recording of the sealings in the E. Wing and their precise location are set out by M.A.V.G. in Section 2. There are other aspects and difficulties which deserve consideration even at the cost of considerable repetition, all the more so since M.R.P. is much more suspicious of the value of many of Evans's later changes and has doubts about the precise locations ascribed to some of the sealings in M.A.V.G.'s lists. Evans, too, in the end may have found his own records too confusing and been led to adopt the simplified presentation of them in *PM* IV.602–5, an 'Archives Deposit' (C) and an 'East Hall Borders Deposit' (D).

   An early error is to be seen on his sketch plan of 1901 (*AE/NB* 1901.42) on which he marked sealings as having been found in the most southerly or 4th bay of the Corridor of the Bays, situated immediately north of the Grand Staircase, whereas they had in fact been discovered on the landing of the staircase, just to the south.

Perhaps after consulting Mackenzie's Day Book in drafting the customary Annual Report, he realized his mistake and deleted his crosses placed in the bay and substituted others, correctly, on the landing. They remain correctly located on his sketch plan for 1902 (*AE/NB* 1902.1 reproduced *OKT* plate XX). There the matter might rest were it not that it had meanwhile affected his recording, as we shall see, while he still on several occasions repeated his error in later years, e.g. *PM* III.316–17 where one sealing is ascribed to the Corridor of the Bays and listed under MM III in the Index Volume, the date of the vases there.

While still under this misapprehension, Evans had made three lists of sealings which he had ascribed to the Gallery of the Bays, 4th Bay, but, after seeing this to be mistaken, changed to Stair Landing or Landing of the Seal Impressions, though in two instances omitting to cross out his initial heading (PLATES 40 right, 42 top left and 41).

So far the position is clear, a simple mistake later rectified. But then complications arise from further alterations at a later stage to the headings given to R8–31 where Landing is rewritten more clearly with '(Earlier Deposit L.M.1)' added below. On the other side of the heading Evans added, apparently at the same time, '(See too below for others found nr. E. door of Hall of Colonnades)', presumably referring to his record the next year of R67–84, to be considered below. Apart from the curious use of 'too', there is no reason to doubt that all the sealings from R2 to R37 were really found on the landing, and are so listed by M.A.V.G. Another apparently contemporary addition are the words 'under blocking' beside R8 and R9 which, as M.A.V.G. observes, are apparently encircled, suggesting that this location refers only to them. If so, Evans misunderstood what he had intended at some later stage. For, when copying out and collecting together his various scattered entries, which must have been post-1928 because of a reference to *PM* II, he headed this page of his notes Gallery of the Bays and Earlier Deposit, adding below '(landing & under blocking)', so giving it general application. We shall have cause to return to these notes later, while the addition of the words under blocking will be considered in the comment on Rs 8 and 9. It is of interest, however, to see that he retained the original heading of Gallery of Bays on one page of these notes and Gallery of Bays, Bay 4 on the second since this continuation of his old error may have led to further subsequent mistakes. An instance of this is in *PM* IV.520–1 and fn. 1 where Evans talks of 'a palatial deposit at Knossos of MM III-LM I date' explained in the footnote as 'an earlier deposit of seal impressions found at the West end of the E.-W. Corridor, extending under the later blocking of the entrance to the Corridor of the Bays'.

Greater problems arise with the entry of R38–51 where, though not reflected in the order of her numbering, M.A.V.G. has concluded, with good reason, that the right hand page with the heading was written first (i.e. PLATE 43 right, containing R67–84) and was continued across to the left hand page (i.e. PLATE 43 left with R38–51) with its heading 'Part of Treasury Dept.' This must be a later addition, as she observes, since that room was excavated near the end of the 1902 season and even then was probably initially dubbed 'the Secretary's bureau', as on the later entry for R88–99. In that case, the heading on the right hand page should originally have applied to both pages, Evans having started his entries on that side. The real difficulties arise from Evans's subsequent amendments and especially the purpose of his later subdivision of the left hand page by a line drawn across it. It might seem at first that help in interpreting them might be found in his late notes. His page headed Demon Seals is clearly very selective but includes examples not only from the right hand page, R67–84 (as well as the sealing numbered by M.A.V.G. R52) but also a selection from those below the line drawn across the left hand page, R45–50. Which brings us to the original heading 'Gallery S. of Gt. Tank system and below nr. E. door of Hall of Colonnades'. This was deleted subsequently apart from the word Gallery, and 'of the Demon Seals' substituted, correctly as being its eventual name, and after the Great Tank system had been recognized to be the light well to the Grand Staircase. However, the second half of the title was also deleted including the note below it '(several with tablets but not belonging to "burnt tablet" deposit)', an addition which can only refer to those in the Hall of the Colonnades since no tablets are recorded from the Gallery where the sealings occurred at a high level, hence the 'below' for those near the E. door which may even have been at floor level. These are marked on Evans's plan of 1902. This raises the question of whether the deletion of the second part of the heading was deliberate or accidental. Later, at least, Evans took it as being intentional, for in his notes headed Demon Seals he redrew a selection of seals on both pages, as described above, but only from those below the dividing line on the left hand page. In other words he interpreted the entries, differently from M.A.V.G., taking no account of the downward pointing arrow below the words '(below E.-W. Passage) nr. E. door of Hall of Colonnades'. But was he correct? The encircling line around R52 extracting it from the entries on the right hand page, i.e. those from the Gallery, and adding it to those below the line on the opposite page only makes sense if the latter were not from the Gallery but were, indeed, from the doorway in the Hall. So, I conclude that Evans misinterpreted what his annotations intended. If so, it might be clearer to ascribe R45–50 and R52 to the deposit within the Hall of Colonnades near the E. door, rather than to the Lower East–West Corridor as M.A.V.G., though the difference in distance is marginal.

This leaves to be considered the sketches of Rs 38–44 above the dividing line with the heading 'Part of Treasury Dept.' discussed earlier. In his notes, Evans redrew R44 and described R43 as '?Heraldic lions and palm' failing to recognize that the latter depicted a corresponding Master of Animals motive. These he ascribed to Nr. E. door of Hall of Colonnades. He takes no account of Rs 38–42 which leaves these in limbo unless the centrally placed annotation 'Hall of Colonnades (cf. R. of Lily Crown', with its faint upward and downward arrows, was intended to apply to all the sealings, as M.A.V.G. concludes. This, however, hardly explains the comparison with the Room of the Lily Crown, which can only mean the Room of the Clay signet. Nothing is clear, and I can only suggest that this comparison indeed refers to the clay matrix and that Evans forgot his intention to put there a cross, referring to his addition at the very bottom of the page 'x (also two impressions of the signet with cup and orb)' with below '(burnt found in hall-associated with burnt tablets)', M.A.V.G.'s number R51. Whether any value should be placed on the general heading of this page of 'Part of Treasury Dept.', though a later addition, must remain uncertain. It could either have a specific reference to the Treasury Room (or the presumed Archive Room above it) or merely adopted vaguely of the region as a whole as Evans uses it for his Deposit C.

Fortunately no complications attach to subsequent entries for R53–66 and R100–105, all given specific locations, as well as R85–87 straightforwardly ascribed to the Gallery of the Demon Seals (PLATE 42).

R88–99 are ascribed jointly to the Wooden Staircase (i.e. Demon Seal deposit) as well as the 'Secretary's bureau', i.e. the Lair, Treasury or Archive Room to give it its various later names. The added comment 'Same deposit as passage' (i.e. the dog-leg corridor E. of the Wooden Staircase and N. of the Treasury) with the additional observation 'Two dogs or wolves on base very frequent' could imply that impressions of R88 occurred there too, though it might equally be a general observation regarding the spread of sealings over the whole region.

As remarked at the beginning, it is hardly surprising that Evans, faced with the complications and confusions of his records, decided for his final account of the sealings from the E. Wing in *PM* IV.561–9 to short cut the problems he had encountered by allocating them to two main deposits, his C and D with lists on pp. 602–5. Though even in so doing his allocation of sealings to Deposit C – a general spread originating from his presumed Room of the Archives, and Deposit D – the Landing extending into the E-W Corridor, contains its own confusions, as reference to M.A.V.G.'s lists of these two 'deposits' and their corresponding sealings will readily reveal.

In so simplifying issues, he was probably justified since, apart from the deposit on the landing, it is clear from the excavation record that with the collapse of the upper structures the sealings were scattered, like the tablets, over the whole region. There can be no real doubt that all the deposits were contemporary and were preserved by the same destructive event, which makes Evans's occasional ambivalence in earlier volumes of *PM* the more incomprehensible.

Evans's inclusion of otherwise unrecorded sealings in his C list with the further additions given by M.A.V.G. of her Ca–c and Cd on the basis of their entry in the Inventory and/or of the location given them elsewhere in *PM*, raises doubts. However, there is supporting evidence at least for the provenance of Cb (Her. s. 661) in a footnote (2) to *PM* III.474 where the comparison made must refer to that sealing, which is located in the Room of the Archives. The other information contained there is of considerable importance: for Evans states that it was found 'in a heap of fragments' (presumably from that room) 'first examined in 1922'. So he may then have made another list, now lost, which would account for these additions.

R1

R51

R54

Evans's note beside Q22 (PLATE 40) is later than his sketch of it; his use of 'then' makes this certain. It is not, however, clear that he is referring to another sealing in addition to those of R51, which I have suggested above may have been ascribed to the Hall of the Colonnades. M.A.V.G. cogently argues that only Her. s. 281 (PLATE 17) is both a 'part of ... impression' and shows the handles of the cup clearly, which is the main point of his comment.

With the lack of any sketches to enable certain identifications, it seemed best to place the examples together on PLATES 7–8 with additional sealings at PLATE 17.

The upper drawing on PLATE 28, a less well preserved example, Ox. 1938. 1015a, appears only in *PM* IV.597 plate 591(a) where it was chosen as an example of a nodule the back of which bore the impression of wicker-work which Evans wished to illustrate, plate 591(c). The lower drawing, used on several occasions, is, as Evans states, a composite reconstruction from both the impressions and the clay matrix, Q22.

In *PM* II.768–9, Evans compares these sealings with those impressed with a similar scene found at Zakro, and details the differences. In that same passage, he again 'adjusts' the stratigraphical context of the matrix, perhaps influenced by his dating 'earliest LM I phase' (*sic* LM IB) of the Zakro sealings and their context. Discussed also by J. Betts, *Kadmos* 6 (1967) 20.

R2

Evans commissioned another drawing which he did not publish. See Gill, *BSA* 60 (1965) plate 6. Dated Younger, '1450–1400'.

R3

Dated Younger, '1410–1385'.

R4

Dated Younger, '1410–1385'.

R5

Her. s. 247 (PLATE 19) would suit the description of 'lower part of bull', a possibility strengthened by its inventory number within the sequence of the early R sealings.

R6

The comment, damaged by the cutting out for drawing of R13 behind it, on PLATE 40 can be mostly restored from Evans's later notes which read 'Part of cattle piece, fine work'. His sketch for a possible restoration of the design was shown to be mistaken by the finding of Her. s. 1000 and 1005 = Betts nos. 51–2 who gives a description and sketch, not repeated here. The impressions, especially Her. s. 212–13 are notable examples of the lack of care taken in making a full impression, as well as variations in the quality of the clay. For the comment '?Earlier deposit' see the note on R8 and R9 below. Dated Kenna, p.14 no. 55, 'LM II early'; Younger, '1410–1385'.

R7

Evans's note under his sketch '?P.of M. III' must have been added after its publication in 1930. It is clearly meant to refer to *PM* III.317 fig. 20, the sealstone from

Zafer Papoura T.36 (= CMS II 3 no. 40) which closely resembles the sealing and led Evans there to confuse the drawings of the two and allocate both to the E. Wing deposits. The context of the seal is LM II-IIIA 1. Dated Younger, 'early 15th century'.

R8
R9

Evans's note beside these of 'Landing-Earlier Deposit LM.I' with below 'under blocking' has been discussed by M.A.V.G and M.R.P. above. Even if it arose from a confused recollection of his earlier mislocation of the sealings found on the landing to the Corridor of the Bays with its MM III pottery, this hardly accounts for the comment 'under blocking', i.e. of the doorway into the Corridor, otherwise unattested in the NB's. It looks like another case of 'wishful thinking'. The other note there 'MM IIIb', presumably his dating of the signet which impressed R8 and R9, must be late since this classification does not appear until *PM* II in 1928. The other annotation 'Do.' (i.e. ditto) 'variant', appears to refer to R9. Discussed with R37 by Betts, *Kadmos* 6 (1967) 26–7 whose drawing of R8, fig. 11, is reproduced here on PLATE 28. Dated Younger, 'early 15th century'.

R10

Dated Younger, 'early 15th century'.

R12
R14
R27

Not recognized as being impressions from the same seal. All placed together here on PLATE 9 with photographic reconstruction at PLATE 25. See M.A.V.G. for identifications. She has suggested to M.R.P. that the signet appears to have been damaged at top right, as illustrated here. As in the case of the unprovenanced Her. s. 147 (PLATE 19), more detailed later study of the sealings would have provided Evans with this group as a further example of the 'impaled triangle' motive, regarded by him as a 'symbol of sacral import' (PM III 316). Dated Younger, '1410–1385'.

R13

The faint annotation reads Eph. Arch. 1888 plate X,36. Considered by J. Sakellarakis in his discussion of bull sacrifices in *PZ* 45 (1970) 217 no. B3. Dated Younger, 'first half of 15th century'.

R17

Evans failed to recognize that R17, annotated '3 bulls', was impressed by the same signet as R25 and R29, which were identified as moufflons. His sketch of R17 (PLATE 41) with 4 examples, may have been partly completed with the addition of Her. s. 232, clearly the impression from a different seal as we can now see. R29 was drawn and published as though it were a complete impression (PLATE 29). Photographic reconstruction at PLATE 25. Dated Younger, '1450–1385'.

R18

Evans comments 'Rock crystal Z.P.Tomb', i.e. Her. s. 836 = CMS II 3,21 from Zafer Papoura Tomb 36, which he did not illustrate in *PreT*. His later substitution for this in his notes 'cf. Crystal with LM II pottery', i.e. *PM* IV.588 fig. 583 with 'mature LM II' pottery, and *PM* IV. Suppl. plate LVj, is much more pertinent as, too, is N1 with its engraving of the muzzle. Dated Younger, 'First half of the 15th century'.

R19

Impressed by the same signet as R30, with several duplicates placed together on PLATE 10, and a photographic reconstruction at PLATE 25.

R20

Dated Younger, '1410–1385'.

R21

Dated Younger, '1410–1385'.

R23

Dated Younger, '1550–1500'.

R32

Both impressions were drawn and published by Evans (PLATE 29). Differences in the two inaccurate drawings led him to think they were variants, *PM* IV.607. A yet more inaccurate, not to say imaginative drawing was not used, Gill, *BSA*

60 (1965) plate 5. Photographic reconstruction at PLATE 25. Dated Kenna, p.43 no. 7, 'LM II'.

R36    Dated Younger, '1350–1300' an opinion he has withdrawn, as he has kindly informed me.

R37    Discussed and illustrated by Betts, *Kadmos* 6 (1967) 36 and fig. 8 (not repeated here) in conjunction with R8 and similar sealings from Zakro and Ayia Triadha. Dated Younger, '1530–1485'.

R38    Dated Kenna, p.43 no. 50, 'LM II late'; Younger, '1410–1385'.

R43
R44    A surprising blind spot on the part of Evans, in failing to recognize that it and its duplicate (presumably Her. s. 219) depicted a Master of Animals with attendant lions, especially since he owned and had published at an early stage a sealstone with an almost identical scene, *JHS* 21 (1901) 65 and fig. 43, reproduced on the title page without the mistaken ground lines, now Ash. Mus. 1938, 1054 = Kenna, *Cretan Seals* 9P, plate 18. It was not reproduced in *PM*. M.A.V.G. assures me that Her. s. 218 was recognizably the sealing sketched by Evans for R44 (PLATE 43): it is now very abraded. Had Evans commissioned the sealings to be drawn, he might have reconstructed the design (as at PLATE 25). As it is, he was misled by his initial sketch of R43 when making his later notes, and added then the description '?Heraldic lions and palm'. Dated Younger, '1410–1385'.

R40    'Dog seizing agrimi' would suit well Her. s. 1549 (PLATE 24).

R45    Her. s. 1044 = Betts 28; his drawing is not repeated here. Dated Younger, '1410–1385'.

R46    Noted as being, rather unusually, an amygdaloid, as, too, for K6, but not recognized as being duplicates. Dated Younger for K6, '1500–1475'.

R49    Photographic reconstruction at PLATE 25. Dated Younger, '1550–1500'.

R50    Photographic reconstruction at PLATE 25. In his later notes, Evans annotated '?Zakro', a similarity with a sealing from Zakro which is discussed in *PM* IV.521, where Evans apparently disagrees with Hogarth's opinion that the latter are 'exact replicas of the Knossian type'. Evans again repeats his misrepresentation that the Knossos examples were found in a deposit of MM III-LM I date. This is expanded in fn. 1 as 'the earlier deposit of seal impressions found at the West end of the E.W. Corridor, extending under the later blocking of the entrance to the Corridor of the Bays'. Dated Kenna, p.43 no. 50, 'LM II late'.

R52    Photographic reconstruction at PLATE 25.

R61    Dated Kenna, p.43 no. 46, 'LM II early'.

R66    For the reasons to date this sealing from a Cypriot cylinder to around 1400 BC, see *OKT 72* and fn. 2.

R69    Dated Younger, 'late 15th century'.

R74    Evans's sketch is a composite one, as is the photographic reconstruction at PLATE 25, which includes Her. s. 311/6 sketched by Evans for R97, a duplicate misunderstood by Evans to represent a dog (PLATE 44).

R75    Her. s. 1603, an identification not known at the time to M.R.P. and so not photographed.

R80     Interpreted by Evans as 'pt. of Minotaur with star' (PLATE 43), a small fragment.

R81     The Demon seals which eventually gave the Wooden Staircase its final name. Evans marks '18 pieces' beside his sketch. Not all the identified nodules are illustrated here but additional ones are given on PLATE 17. Dated Kenna, p.43 no. 13, 'LM II Early'.

R83     Dated Younger, '1350–1300' but an opinion, as he has kindly informed me, he has now withdrawn.

R86     Dated Younger, '1500–1475'.

R88     'Very frequent'. Additional examples at PLATE 18 with photographic reconstruction at PLATE 26. It is notable that with so many examples, only one is reasonably complete. Evans's original 'wolves or dogs' become 'collared dogs' by *PM* IV. Kenna, p.44 no. 8 (wrongly ascribed to the Little Palace, following an error by Evans who placed it in his 'E Deposit', no. 8) comments, 'These are lions and possibly LH II work'. Dated Younger, '1410–1385'.

R89     For a drawing prepared by Evans but not used, see Gill, *BSA* 60 (1965) plate 7, not repeated here.

R92     Evans's comment beside his sketch (PLATE 44) 'cf. Zakro hoard' seems to have led him to imagine a stratigraphical context for which there is no other evidence: *PM* I.713 fn. 2 'Found with other early seal-impressions underneath the later "service" staircase of the Domestic Quarter'.

R94     Photographic reconstruction at PLATE 26.

R95     Evans's description 'Deer seized by lion? amid naturalistic foliage', of which he notes 'several', admirably suits Her. s. 1001 (PLATE 21) = Betts 63, with his drawing not repeated here, though it would imply that Evans misinterpreted the impression. See note on C41 below.

R100    Dated Kenna, p.43 no. 21, 'LM II'.

R101    Dated Younger, '1410–1385'.

R102    Evans aptly comments 'like modern crest' (PLATE 44).

R104    Countermarked; Gill, p.5. Sealing apparently lost but the countermark is recorded by Evans at PLATE 44.

R105    Dated Younger, '1410–1385'. Evans comments 'school of three dolphins perh. originally 6'.

R107    Not photographed.

C1–68   Some doubt about the correct provenance inevitably arises in cases where the only evidence is limited to ascriptions in *PM*, especially as three at least belong to deposits elsewhere. The original drawings are not marked with their find spots, while slips in Evans's memory are not unusual. However, it may be that the finding in 1922, mentioned by Evans, of apparently previously unprocessed sealings, may have been the occasion on which he selected out certain ones for drawing, without, it seems, listing them or recording the remainder. It could even have been at that time that he added additional numbers of examples beside some sealings recorded early on. See last para. of note to R2–99 above.

C9        Dated Younger, '1525–1475', his Cretan Popular Group. However, W-D. Niemeier
          in *Minoan Socity*, eds. O. Krzyszkowska and L. Nixon (Bristol 1983) p. 220 and fn. 38
          maintains that it is related to seals and sealings of 'late appearance' and cites
          parallels in support of this classification.

C10       A jar stopper according to J. Weingarten, *Oxford Journal of Archaeology* 7 (1988) 22.
          Dated Kenna, p.43 no. 10, 'LM or LH II'.

C11       Photographic reconstruction at PLATE 26. Dated Kenna, p.43 no. 11, 'LM II';
          Younger, 'LM IIIA 1'.

C15       Dated Kenna, p.43 no. 15, 'LM II'. This is one of the two sealings, referred to in
          Section 1, as being given a late dating by Younger, who ascribes it to his Rhodian
          Hunt Group with suggested dates of 1350–1300.

C38       Dated Kenna, p.43 no. 38, '?LM IB'.

C41       The drawing at PLATE 30 is fairly certainly a composite drawing, but of what? It
          has not been identified. I have toyed with the idea that it could be based on R95 and
          its 'several' duplicates also unidentified. This would imply that Evans mis-
          understood the actual scene; he was clearly uncertain. However, his comment
          'amid naturalistic foliage' suggests something rather unusual. Could it be that it
          is a conflation of Her. s. 145, 1001 (on which the lowered horns of the left hand
          bull are visible), and Her. s. 1375 for the palm trees, with the original of R95
          which still escapes identification, as well as other sealings, lost or among those
          without provenance. If Her. s. 321 (R37) also belonged, it would place the signet
          in the Domestic Quarter. If there is anything in this, the peculiar baseline of the
          drawing would be the stepped basis visible on 145 and 1001, much of the foliage
          would have been left out and the stance of the left hand bull's forelegs inaccurately
          portrayed. C41 would then be a doublet. M.A.V.G. will have none of it!

C42       Dated Kenna, p.43 no. 42, 'LM II late'.

C43       Dated Kenna, p.43 no. 43, 'LM II late'.

C45       Dated Kenna, p.43 no. 45, 'LM II', apparently from its drawing in *PM* IV.564 fig.
          533 since it has subsequently been lost.

C51       Dated Younger, '1410–1385'.

Cb        See note to C2–99, last para. above.

Cc        Dated Younger, '1410–1385'.

S1        The original apparently lost. The photograph at PLATE 16 is reproduced from that
          used by Evans for *SM* II plate 88. The countermark is drawn by Evans, PLATE 45.
          Evans recognized that the sealing was impressed by the same signet as ones from the
          Arsenal, the Vc series, on which see note below.

S2        '& head', words accidentally omitted from PLATE 45 but included on *OKT* plate
          XXIII.

U1–117    The only sealings in HM are those put aside for drawing at various stages, several
          not subsequently published (PLATES 30–1). Some 100 sealings have been lost or
          stolen. The numbers of shapes and motives given with apparent precision by
          Kenna, pp.40–1, can have been based for the greatest part on Evans's sketches
          only, though this is not stated.

U1–24 were recorded later than U25–116 and are titled Little Palace instead of the earlier nomenclature for the building, the House of the Fetishes.

| | |
|---|---|
| U7 | Dated Younger, '1450–1425'. |
| U54/117 | Dated Younger, '1410–1385'. |
| U56 | Dated Kenna, p.43 no. 1, 'LM II'. |
| U86 | Dated Kenna, p.44 no. 10, 'LM IIIA', from the drawing as the original has been lost. |
| U112 | Dated Kenna, p.44 no. 10, 'LM II and LH II', reflecting his belief that the horse is a secondary engraving and a Mainland alteration (p.50 and fn. 54). |
| U117 | See U54 above. |
| E19 | Dated Kenna, p.44, 'LM II'. |
| V | Evans must have made notes on the sealings in 1904, the year of their excavation, prior to the account given of them in his Annual Report in *BSA* 10 (1903–4) 60–2. None has been found. |
| Va | Additional examples are given on PLATE 18. The plumage drawn on the wings of the birds, PLATE 31, are an imaginative addition. M.A.V.G. has discussed the vertical fracture and mend on the seal and on J2: reference given in the note there, above. |
| Vc Vd | Evans believed that the two series were impressed by the same seal and that the indistinct impression on some of them (the Vc series) was due to subsequent handling when the countermark was incised. This is not the case and the one seal, responsible too for S1, as Evans recognized, *PM* IV.618, must have been very worn.<br><br>   The impressions are discussed by Kenna, p.49 and fig. 7, where he gives a reconstruction of the seal responsible for the Vd series, with perhaps greater definiteness than the impressions allow. Dated p.48, 'LM II late'. |
| Vc | For the countermark and endorsement on Her. s. 119 and Her. s. 401, see Evans, *PM* IV.616 fig. 603, and Gill, fig. 2, 7 and 9. For the countermark on Her. s. 403, see Evans, *loc. cit.* and Gill, fig. 3, 17. Additional examples are given at PLATE 18. |

*Sealings without provenance*

These are a selection only, which is far from complete. For duplicates within them, see M.A.V.G.'s Concordance A and Addendum in Section 2.

   The drawings, too, are selective and do not include many of those published in Betts, *BSA* 62 (1967) 27–45 which should be consulted, too, for his descriptions.

| | |
|---|---|
| 138 | See note to N5 above. |
| 145 | See note to J5 above. |
| 255 1529 | A combination recognized and published by I. Pini, *Philia Epi* Vol. 1, 303f. and plate 52. I am grateful to him for permission to reproduce his drawing at PLATE 32. Photographic reconstruction at PLATE 26. |
| 328 1008 | Composite photographic reconstruction at PLATE 26. Her. s. 1008 = Betts 66 whose drawing is not reproduced here. |

369          See M.A.V.G.'s remarks in Section 2 under Little Palace and her reconstruction of
             the design of the signet at PLATE 32(b).

370          Photographic reconstruction at PLATE 26. The drawing on the Frontispiece is a
381          rather idealized reconstruction and assumes that the signet was a gold ring. As
             M.A.V.G., who has participated in the reconstruction, remarks, the signet could
             be an amydaloid.

416          See note above to N8 which M.R.P. believes to be this sealing.

650–660      See M.A.V.G.'s introduction to Section 2 above for the possible provenance of these
             and other sealings. The drawings at PLATE 32 were commissioned by Evans but
             not published by him.

660          Photographic reconstruction at PLATE 26 and in a drawing at PLATE 32 which
             Evans did not publish.

998          = Betts no. 45.

1001         = Betts no. 63. A possible duplicate of R95, see note on C41 above.

1002         = Betts no. 62.

1003         = Betts no. 44.

1004         = Betts no. 64.

1006         = Betts no. 43; his drawing reproduced at PLATE 32.

1007         = Betts no. 47; his drawing reproduced at PLATE 32.

1008         = Betts no. 66. See note to Her. s. 328 above. Dated Younger, 'c.1530–1480'.

1009         = Betts no. 57. Dated Younger, 'c.1530–1480'.

1010         = Betts no. 54.

1012         = Betts no. 56.

1014         = Betts no. 46.

1019         = Betts no. 58.

1022         = Betts no. 49.

1026         = Betts no. 32; his drawing reproduced at PLATE 32.

1027         = Betts no. 40.

1028         = Betts no. 19.

1030         = Betts no. 29; his drawing reproduced at PLATE 32.

1032         = Betts no. 8.

1034         = Betts no. 18.

1033         = Betts no. 10; his drawing reproduced at PLATE 32.

1035        = Betts no. 14.

1037        = Betts no. 13; his drawing reproduced at PLATE 32. Dated Younger, '*c*.1530–1480'.

1038        = Betts no. 7.

1040        = Betts no. 3; his drawing reproduced at PLATE 32.

1041        = Betts no. 31. See note to N4 above. Dated Younger, '*c*.1530–1480'.

1045        = Betts no. 41.

1198        See note on Q5 which M.R.P. believes to be this sealing.

1270        = Betts no. 16; his drawing reproduced at PLATE 32.

1275        = Betts no. 12. Combined with Her. s. 369 in M.A.V.G.'s drawing at PLATE 32(b).

1276        = Betts no. 24.

1277        = Betts no. 23; his drawing reproduced at PLATE 23. Not photographed.

1293        = Betts no. 30.

1375        See note to N3; a possible candidate.

1393        See note to Q10 above.

1529        See note on Her. s. 255 above.

1546–8      See comment on N1–13 above. Found with tablets ascribed to the Room of the Chariot Tablets.

1549        See note on R40 above.

The unnumbered sealing on PLATES 24 and 32, is published by J. Betts, *BSA* 74 (1979) 274–5 and plate 40 and dated by him, 'early 15th century' or earlier.

# Section 4

# Some aspects of the sealings: their dating, association with tablets and their condition

M.R. POPHAM

## 1. *Dating*

Any account of the dating of the sealings must give pride of place to Evans himself. Near the end of his lifetime interest and study of Minoan glyptics, he gave in the last volume of *Palace of Minos* a comprehensive survey of the subject, which included his account of the latest sealings (*PM* IV.591–618). He, of course, had no doubt about the date of the destruction which had preserved them, and, on this basis concluded 'It seems reasonable to infer that the majority of the sealings belonged to the epoch immediately preceding that historical landmark', adding the necessary caution 'that the signets themselves that had impressed the clay nodules might in certain cases have been considerably older than the impressions preserved' (*PM* IV.599). While deploring the loss of 'the forceful natural spirit' (of the previous century) 'which is rarely visible in the intaglio designs of the last Palatial Age as we see them reflected in the clay impressions' (p. 601), there is no hint that he was in any way worried that they might be later than the date to which he ascribed them. Such comments as he occasionally makes in his notes mostly relate to the quality of the engraving, ranging from 'good' to 'fair' to 'poor' or 'rough', as for instance on PLATE 45, without chronological implications.

Then there was a hiatus until 1960 when Kenna in *Cretan Seals*, as part of his overall survey of Cretan glyptics, considered the sealings, or rather such as Evans had illustrated as well as others in the Ashmolean Museum. He was able, also, to take account of the publication of additional material, including the sealings from Sklavokambos and the seals in the LM II Warrior Graves at Knossos; he was permitted, too, to study and refer to seals found in tombs excavated by Platon, which were still unpublished. In general his account builds upon that of Evans, sharing with him an ambivalence about the date of the deposits of sealings from Zakro and Ayia Triadha.[1] Unlike Evans, his survey continued into LM III. Another addition was the inclusion of a list of 30 sealings with particular seals which he considered to be 'obviously related and in some cases may ultimately have come from the same hand or school' (p. 58).

The renewed interest in the sealings which resulted from the dispute over the date of the final destruction of the palace, has already been outlined in Section 1.

The initial defence by Kenna of the traditional dating in Appendix 3 of *OKT*, resulted in an attack on his competence, which prompted him to reply and expand his earlier account in an article of 1964 in *Kadmos* 3, 29–57. He there first set out the basis for the accepted chronological development of the seals, taking account of shapes, motives, materials and style, and of dated deposits. He then went on to consider 35 sealings, which had been illustrated by Evans, and a further 15 which were especially relevant to the dispute in being countersigned or endorsed with Linear B characters. These he mostly ascribed to LM II seals, but allotted a few somewhat later to LM IIIA. This is not surprising, since by then the opinion that the Knossos destruction took place when LM IIIA 1 pottery was in use was becoming the accepted view, with its consequence of a slight lowering of the date from 1400 to around 1375 BC.[2] This revision of Evans's classification meant that burials in the Kalyvia cemetery near Phaestos could also be included. Parallels between some of the Knossos sealings and seals from those burials were drawn by Kenna who even suggested, implausibly, that some of those seals might have been pillaged from the Knossos palace itself after its destruction.

He was, of course, concerned to counter Palmer's view of an LM IIIB destruction. Having studied the seals as well as the sealings in Herakleion Museum, he maintained that there were at least 300 LM IIIB seals in that collection, 130 of which came from Knossos and its neighbour-hood, and concluded that 'no sealing with a type comparable with the stones of LM IIIB has yet been found among the Late Palace sealings' (p. 39, repeated p. 50).

Supporters of Palmer's LM IIIB date for the destruction have so far not seriously challenged Kenna's conclusions but have concentrated their defence on emphasizing that the dating relates to the signets and not to the sealings which they impressed, adding that the use of older seals can be paralleled on Mainland Greece and especially at Pylos.[3]

Individual sealings have featured subsequently in studies principally concerned with seals, some of which are referred to in Section 3. Additionally one entire deposit, that from the Room of the Chariot Tablets, consisting of seven impressed sealings with a possible addition of two others, has been given provisional dating by I. Pini and J. Younger who are in basic agreement that none are later than LM IIIA with the majority being LM IIIA 1 or slightly earlier.[4] The latest date ascribed to the sealings overall, or rather to the signets which impressed them is LM IIIA and this, too, is the opinion of I. Pini, who, apart from his expertise, is familiar with all the sealings which he has studied in preparation for their eventual publication in the CMS series.[5]

The fullest consideration of the sealings since Kenna's study is that included in a series of articles by J. Younger who has sought to ascribe seals and their impression on sealings to stylistic groups, which are then, in turn, assigned ranges of dates for their manufacture based on the contexts in which examples of the groups have appeared.[6] It is mostly limited to those Knossian sealings given a context and identified by Gill in her article and to others pub-lished elsewhere, but his opinions are based on acquaintance with the actual sealings or on drawings and photographs in the CMS archive which he was permitted to study. His conclu-sion in the last article is that with a very few exceptions the latest stylistic group recognized on the sealings belongs to his 'Spectacle-Eye Group' and that its members were responsible for more Knossos sealings than any other stylistic group.[7] Their earliest context is in LM IIIA 1 burials while the final date for their manufacture is, somewhat hypothetically, placed at 1385 BC, i.e. still within the LM IIIA 1 stage. His exceptions later in date are four, proposed with varying degrees of probability and one, only, has an established context, Her. s. 297 = K5.[8] The two groups to which they are assigned (his Rhodian Hunt Group and Central Islands Sanctuaries Group) are clearly difficult to date since most occur in contexts where they are fairly certainly prized heirlooms. His mid- fourteenth century date for their appearance is based more on stylistic affinities with earlier groups than on contextual evidence. That the ear-liest of these groups could well have been made before the 1475 date of the Knossian destruc-tion, would be difficult to refute on present evidence and might be thought to be more likely, given his earlier dating of the 150 or so others with which they are to be associated. That number, circumscribed by previous publication, has now been considerably increased by this present work making a fuller, more comprehensive, study possible in the future.

In any such reassessments, there are several aspects with a mainly chronological significance which, it is suggested, might deserve fuller attention than has so far been generally given. More consideration, for instance, might be given to the condition of the signets being used, as far as their impression will allow. Margaret Gill has already shown that two seals had been mended after breakage, and has suggested that another was chipped.[9] The seal responsible for many of the sealings from the Arsenal and one from the Corridor of the Sword Tablets seems to have been seriously abraded, presumably made of steatite,[10] the relatively soft nature of which is made very apparent by the enlarged stringholes on many seals, especially those in LM/LH IIIB and IIIC contexts, when replacements may have been difficult, if not impossible, to obtain. Even more liable to wear must have been the gold signets, an aspect, for instance, clearly to be seen on one from Kalyvia, only slightly visible on another from Isopata, but absent on that from Sellopoulo, indicating the probability that it is near contemporary with the LM IIIA I pottery with which it was associated.[11]

### 2. *Sealings and tablets*

The conjunction of sealings and tablets is, of course, a commonplace observation, nowhere more apparent than in the E–W Corridor of the Domestic Quarter, but their precise relationship is far from clear.

If the sealings had been used principally to secure containers holding tablets, as Evans appears to have thought, it might be expected that some numerical coincidence between the two classes of object would result. That this is not so will be immediately apparent from the table below in which the numbers given of tablets and of major scribes is approximate only, and the exact number of sealings is sometimes in doubt, but they are sufficiently accurate to make comparisons valid.

| Region | | Tablets | | Sealings | |
|---|---|---|---|---|---|
| | Total | Hands | Major Scribes | Total | Types |
| W. Mags. and Long Corridor | c.200 | 30 | 7+ | c.16 | 15? |
| R. of Chariot Tablets | c.140 | 12 | 4? | 11 | 11 |
| R. of Column Bases | c.56 | 12 | 2 | 2 | 1 |
| R. of Jewel Fresco | c.20 | 8 | 2 | 18 | 14? |
| Area of Clay signet | 8? | | | 29? | 22 |
| N. Entrance and area | c.250 | 50 | 17 | 6 | 4 |
| Domestic Quarter | c.450 | 10 | 6 | c.196 | 100+ |
| Corridor of Sword Tablets | 40 | 12 | 4? | 2–3 | 2–3 |
| Arsenal | 92 | 12+ | 6 | 13 | 4 |
| Little Palace | 6+? | | | | c.120?? |

The clearest divergence in numbers and proportions is to be seen in the case of the deposit in the N. Entrance and its immediate area, which produced some 250 tablets but only 6 sealings, two of which are from the same signet. An opposite picture is provided in the region of the S. Basements, with its 35 sealings, of which 17 were impressed by 3 seals, as compared with the 5 (or possibly 8) tablets from the same area. The exact situation in the Little Palace must remain to some extent uncertain, since most of the actual sealings have been lost, and more than the 6 recorded tablets may possibly have been found there; but even so, there can be no doubt that the sealings, of which Evans sketched some 120, vastly outnumbered tablets.

If the enquiry is widened to take into account the number of sealings as compared with the number of scribal hands and 'major hands', as proposed by J-P. Olivier in *Les Scribes de Cnossos*, no relationship at all is apparent in any deposit.

Even making allowance, as we must, for accidental circumstances of preservation, it would appear that the idea that sealings were primarily used to secure containers of tablets cannot be maintained. The picture which emerges is complex and not remotely uniform. In this, no doubt the use of sealings in connection with other objects played a part, probably a major one. One example of such a multiple usage may be discernible in the Arsenal where sealings were found in conjunction with the remains of wooden boxes which could well, as Mackenzie thought, have contained the arrowheads found with them, but other sealings, some distance away, were associated with deposits of tablets.[12]

Fundamental to any enquiry into the purpose of the sealings and the objects they secured, is the condition of the sealings as they were found, an aspect to which we now turn.

### 3. *The condition of the sealings*

'Compared with the impressed nodules of the earlier class, this later material largely consisted in scattered fragments. Indeed, the proportion of perfect seal impressions was very small' (*PM* IV.593). This aspect of the latest Knossian sealings is very apparent to anyone studying them at first hand rather than from the published drawings which sometimes restore the whole design or are the result of a conflation of several incomplete examples. In the same passage, Evans initially ascribes their condition both to their original friable state, being composed of unbaked clay, and to the circumstances whereby they had in most cases clearly fallen from an upper floor.

He was aware, at the same time, that they were considerably more fragmentary than the LM IB sealings from other sites and the MM IIIB ones from the Temple Repositories. To account for this, he fell back on the rather forced explanation that the earlier sealings were of finer clay and were 'well-baked as the result of some special method of treatment' (*PM* IV.593). Though some of the later sealings are somewhat coarse in fabric, it is doubtful whether overall his distinction in quality would stand up to careful scrutiny. He did not expand on what he thought the difference in treatment might be. Moreover, although vases may well break when they fall from an upper storey, it is not very obvious why sealings should suffer the same damage: indeed, the 13 examples from the Arsenal are mostly intact though they too had fallen into a basement from above.

Apparently uneasy at the adequacy of his explanation, Evans went on to add 'The opening of letters or other documents ... naturally accounts for a large amount of the breakage', which, leaving aside for the moment what was sealed, and adding the possibility of resealing and further unsealing, might better account for some of the sealings, for example the 11 examples recorded by Evans of Q2, the 10 of R52, the 18 of R81 and the 'very frequent' occurrence of R88, of which 18 examples have been identified. Despite their numbers, very few of these are near intact and it is noticeable that many of these and others are fractured along the line of the cord around which they were fashioned. True this would be their weakest point, but, equally, it is the natural place to break a sealing deliberately. As a general explanation, however, serious difficulties stand in its way if we are thinking of internal administrative practices and of documents – principally the number of individual seal types represented and the thickness of the cord around which many were fashioned. On the first point, some 100 seals were responsible for the sealings in the deposits of the Domestic Quarter alone, far too many for resident officials; this must mean that in most cases they were impressed by persons operating outside the palace. Some supporting evidence for this may be found in variations in the quality of the clay to be seen even in examples impressed by the same signet e.g. R6 (PLATE 8), which is likely to reflect the nature of the material available at their place of origin.

As to the cord, whose imprint is preserved on many of the sealings, it is usually quite inappropriately thick for the securing of documents written on perishable material. A far finer thread only would be required, of the kind apparent on some LM IB nodules, where such a usage has been convincingly advocated.[13] An alternative view of Evans that they sealed containers of tablets has been examined above and found to be without foundation as a primary function for them. In this connection, his early belief, reasserted later, that such containers were sometimes composed of gypsum slabs is not only highly improbable but fairly clearly a misinterpretation of the evidence due to his initial unfamiliarity with upper, gypsum-paved floors.[14]

On the source of the sealings, Judith Weingarten, in her careful and detailed study of the shapes and types of nodules, has reached the same conclusion, 'most if not all sealings are incoming – stamped by non-resident seal-owners'. As to their purpose, she concludes in the case of the E. Wing that 'they all secured *goods* of various kinds' adding that the majority were 'usually pressed over stout cords certainly securing bulky goods'.[15]

If this interpretation is accepted, we may then go on to ask what goods and why stored in such an unlikely region, which was not without reason called by Evans the Domestic Quarter. Here we meet the same problem raised by me on an earlier occasion – a somewhat improbable picture of activities within the Palace as a whole, of which the sealings and their distribution are but one of the puzzling aspects.[16]

'Bulky goods' may not be a necessary conclusion, and no remains of such survived the conflagration, though it could be argued that all were looted before the palace was set on fire. The same situation is true throughout the building with the exception of the deposits of wheat and Egyptian beans in rooms in the S. Front.[17] A valid alternative would be 'substantial containers', for which there are indications in the form of the remains of wooden chests, at times with bronze hinges and handles, e.g. in the Room of the Chariot Tablets and the Armoury.[18] As for the Domestic Quarter, or E. Wing, no similar evidence was noted and the only surviving large containers are the 3 or so clay pyxis-shaped tubs provided with handles to secure their lids. They, however, come from a passage where no sealings are recorded.[19] There is, clearly, room for further consideration and possibly different interpretations. They may find helpful, as I did, the comments of Margaret Gill which she kindly offered after reading my text.

> I am certain that many of the fragmentary sealings had been broken in antiquity, when the objects they had sealed were opened; others were apparently still intact at the time of the destruction. It is obvious from impressions of various types of string and packaging that the majority of later sealings from the Palace had been attached to a range of articles, the string varying in both thickness and quality, from fine thread through evenly twisted stranded cord and irregularly twisted twine to coarse rope. The nodules were mostly attached around the length of the string, sometimes over a knot (for example, N1 and N6: Her. s. 253 and 111) or next to the knot (Q6: Her. s. 1226/1 with frayed end) and in rare instances over a rectangular slip of wood or reed inserted through the string that may have served to protect a particularly vulnerable article from undue pressure or moisture during sealing (N2: Her. s. 110). Some sealings bear the impression of the container or packaging, where they had been applied to a basketry rim (K2, K11: Her. s. 114–15), wedged into a crevice in the side of a basket (J3: Her. s. 146), or pressed against a smooth flat surface presumably of a box (J2: Her. s. 109); Her. s. 113 (G11) was attached to something with a much rougher surface. The coincidence of several sealings of the same shape, some with impressions of the same seal, and all seemingly having been exposed to a more intense conflagration than other sealings in their vicinity implies that certain large ball-shaped nodules were originally attached to a highly inflammable commodity (R6: Her. s. 212–13). There are also one or two sealings that show no trace of any form of attachment, being unperforated nodules bearing only a seal impression and countermark; these probably performed a completely different function, perhaps acting as chitties to accredit personnel rather than being associated with goods (O7: Her. s. 156 and 224).

Another aspect is of importance to any further consideration, an obvious feature and no new observation; it is apparent that the sealer was indifferent to ensuring that the whole, or even a major part of his signet was impressed, which would have been necessary to make identification of its owner possible. The two impressions of R6, Her. s. 212–3 (PLATE 8) are particularly blatant examples of this.

## NOTES

1. That the Zakro hoard and the destruction of Ayia Triadha belonged to the LM IB stage was remarkably late in being recognized, given the presence of the Marine Style rhyton found with the Zakro sealings and the typical LM IB vases at Ayia Triadha. Even in *PM* IV, well after he had defined many of the characteristics of the LM IB pottery style, Evans still speaks af the MM III–LM IA date of the seal impressions from both sites and the same misdating affected his consideration of stone vases.

2. A definition first proposed by Furumark in *Chronology* pp. 83–5, See also my Appendix A to *OKT* which I made more definite in *Antiquity* 40 (1966) 24–8 and the later *Destruction of the Palace at Knossos* (Lund 1970).

3. E.g. W-D. Niemeier, 'Mycenaean Knossos and the age of Linear B', *SMEA* 23 (1982) 267–8. If the present author is correct in suggesting a very early LH IIIB date for the destruction of the palace at Pylos, the gap between that event and the traditional date for that at Knossos would be considerably narrowed, M. Popham, 'Pylos: Reflections on the date of its destruction and an its Iron Age reoccupation', *Oxford Journal of Archaeology* 10 (1991) 315–24). See also the comment in Section 3 on C9, a specific instance which Niemeier considers to be stylistically late.

4. Their individual dating, as given in J. Driessen, *An Early Destruction in the Palace at Knossos* (Leuven 1990) is as follows, using the abbreviations of P. for I. Pini and Y. for J. Younger; N1 LM IIIA (P), LM I–II (Y); N2 LM IIIA 1 (P), LM IIIA 1 (Y); N6 LM IIIA 1 (P), LM II–IIIA 1 (Y); N7 LM IIIA 1 (P), LM IIIA 1 (Y); N10 LM IB–IIIA 1 (P), LM IIIA 1 (Y); N11 LM I? (P), late MM (Y); N13 LM II–IIIA 1 (P), LM IIIA 1 (Y); ?+ Her. s. 1547 LM IIIA I (P), LM IIIA 1 (Y); Her. s. 1548 LM II–IIIA (P), LM IIIA 1 (Y).

5. An opinion mostly clearly stated in answer to this very point at the Table Ronde on 'La Crète Mycénienne' held at the French Archaeological School in Athens in 1991, the proceedings of which have not yet been published.

6. The most relevant of the series are those in *Kadmos* 25 (1986) 119–40 and 26 (1987) 44–73, with the concordance of the sealings in *Kadmos* 27 (1989) 133–4.

7. *Kadmos* 25 (1986) 131.

8. *Kadmos* 26 (1987) 62, with proposed dating of the groups at pp. 63–4.

9. In CMS , *Die Kretisch-Mykenische Glyptik und ihre Gegenwärtigen Probleme* (1974) 32–6 and plate 32c, and in personal correspondence on the sealings R12 + R14 + R27, PLATE 9 with reconstruction at PLATE 25.

10. See M. Gill in Section 2 on the sealings S1 and Vc, with PLATES 16 and 18.

11. Kalyvia, HM 45 = CMS II 3,114; Isopata, HM 424 = CMS II 3,51 with detailed photograph in *The Proceedings of the 3rd Cretological Conference* (1971) Vol. 1 plate 37; Sellopoulo (J8), BSA 69 (1974) 217–9 and plate 37.

12. *DM/DB* 1904 p. 86, quoted in *OKT* 158; Evans, *BSA* 10 (1903–4) 59–61 and *PM* IV. 615–18.

13. An interpretation put forward by Marinatos in *Minos* 1–2 (1951–2) 39 ff and re-examined by J. Betts in *Kadmos* 6 (1967) 16–40 with photographs of some impressions. See also J. Weingarten in *Oxford Journal of Archaeology* 7 (1988) 12 with references given there.

14. Room of the Column Bases, *AE/NB* and *DM/DB* for 2nd May 1900 and *BSA* 6 (1899–1900) 28; N. Entrance, *AE/NB* 9–12 May 1900 and *BSA* 10 (1903–4) 50 with *PM* III.190; Magazine 8, *PM* IV.671.

15. *Oxford Journal of Arcfiaeology* 7 (1988) 13 with Appendices III–VI.

16. 'The use of the Palace at Knossos at the time of its destruction *c.*1400 BC' in *The Function of the Minoan Palaces* ed. R. Hägg and N. Marinatos (Stockholm 1987) pp. 297–9.

17. The evidence is conveniently summarized by Boardman in *OKT*

18. See *PM* IV.668–9 and earlier reports.

19. Illustrated and discussed by E. Hallager in *The Mycenaean Palace at Knossos* (Stockholm 1977) 92–3. Mackenzie lists 64 fragments of such vessels. The exact location is not quite certain but is most probably that indicated in *The Guide to the Stratigraphical Museum* for N.1.7.

# Section 5

# The seals from the palace and houses

M.R. POPHAM

Though not directly relevant to the purpose of this work, it was thought that a study of the seals and their find-places might make a useful adjunct. The full extent of the problems entailed in this did not become apparent until an advanced stage of its preparation.[1]

It was realized that the finding of some seals in the Palace and houses were recorded in the notebooks, Annual Reports and *PM* but, if anything like complete, their numbers appeared to be remarkably few compared with those found in recent excavations at Knossos.[2] This was all the more surprising in that both Evans and Mackenzie emphasize the care taken in sieving their excavated soil, at least in regions which produced tablets or sealings. Moreover, it was to be expected that Evans, with his long-standing great interest in seals, of which he made his own large private collection, would have been careful about recording and listing them. That this was not so, only slowly emerged.

The sources of information for the seals and their finding, as in the case of the sealings, consist of the dig notebooks of Evans and Mackenzie (*AE/NB*'s and *DM/DB*'s) containing descriptions, sketches or both, supplemented by publications in the Annual Reports and, less reliable, in *PM*. Additionally, there are the entries in the Inventory of Herakleion Museum of seals not otherwise recorded. Unfortunately these usually only state a year though a location is sometimes added, which, as will be seen, is not always correct.

*The Notebooks*

As far as I am aware, these record the finding of nineteen or twenty seals. It seems that at an early stage of the excavations it was agreed that Evans would be responsible for the listing of some classes of objects, including tablets, sealings and seals. At least, after 1902 Mackenzie becomes only a subsidiary source of information. The entries, which have been located, are, in chronological order, the following:

1. *AE/NB* 1900 p.2 (and *DM/DB* 24 March 1900), a 'lentoid bead' 'lion and star & star on rev.', sketched (PLATE 48(a)), found in digging trial trenches on the SE slope of Kephala. Unpublished and apparently lost.

2. *DM/DB* 22 May 1900, in the area of the bull-relief (i.e. N. Entrance), 'an engraved stone (galopetra) with griffin in profile left'. Unpublished, not identifiable and perhaps lost.

3. *AE/NB* 1901 p.1 (and *DM/DB* 4 March 1901), in 9th Magazine, a lentoid described as depicting a man, bull and attacking dog; sketched (PLATE 48(e)). HM 901 = CMS II 3,9. Not published by Evans.

4.      *AE/NB* 1901 p.17 (and *DM/DB* 30 March 1901), a carnelian talismanic seal; sketched and annotated 'NW corner' (i.e. NW corner of the Palace, N. of the W. Magazines (PLATE 48(c)). HM 336 = CMS II 3,12. Not published by Evans.

5.      *AE/NB* 1901 p.17, a cushion seal of chalcedony depicting a fisherman; sketched, original location 'W. of Megaron steps' deleted and 'Outside Palace to N' substituted (PLATE 48(b)). Thus located in *PM* I.677, fig. 497, but becoming NW of site in *PM* IV.500, fig. 440. Ash. Mus. 1938.956 = Kenna 205.

6.      *DM/DB* 4 April 1901, in the region north of the N. end of the Long Corridor, 'a lapis lazula cylinder with figures encased at both ends by a gold disc. The gem was bored from end to end and had small bead ornament round the ends of the boring and round the centre of the gold discs'. Published in *PM* IV.43–4 and figs. 349–50 and located 'just beyond the Western border of the "North Lustral Basin"'. HM 238 = CMS II 2,29.

7.      *AE/NB* 1902 p.19, in or near the Court of the Spout, 'Rough steatite seal griffin'; sketched (PLATE 48(d)). Not published and apparently lost. *DM/DB* 17 February 1902 records the finding of '2 late Mycenaean gems' in the same area, '(one with sphinx)', of which the latter might be the same as Evans's griffin. The other could be a slip for the sealing found also in this area (*AE/NB* 1902 p.18).

8.      *AE/NB* 1902 p.46, pit E. of School Room, a steatite lentoid depicting a woman carrying a double-axe; sketched (PLATE 48(f)). HM 200 = CMS II 3,8. Illustrated first in *PM* I.334, fig. 312 and repeated later; located there in the Court of the Stone Spout and said to come from a MM III stratum.

9.      *DM/DB* 11 May–6 June 1903, NW Area (i.e. NW House), 'Large ivory seal of flat cylindrical shape and bored through from end to end and having a hunting scene on either side'. Ash. Mus. 1968.1844 is the only extant seal which resembles this description except that it has a hunting scene on only one of its two engraved faces; published in *PM* I.197 fig. 145 and *PM* IV.525 fig. 468 and said to have been 'Found in the vicinity of Knossos'. Its genuineness was, however, doubted by Kenna in *Cretan Seals*, was defended by M. Gill in *Kadmos* 6 (1967) 114–18, with a response from Kenna in *Kadmos* 7 (1968) 175f.

10.     *AE/NB* 1903 p.10, W. Building 'House of Fetishes' (i.e. Little Palace), a sketch included among those of sealings annotated 'steatite seal 2 ducks' (PLATE 48(g)), and marked for drawing; = Gill U44. Unpublished and lost.

11.     *AE/NB* 1905 p.12, Procession Corridor and entrance, 'Double Minotaur gem'. Published in Annual Report for 1905 in *BSA* 11 (1904–5) fig. 10 with details of the supplementary investigations then made near the W. Entrance. HM 708 = CMS II 3,10.

12.     *DM/DB* 24–26 April 1908, space between S. wall of Palace and S. House, 'Gem in lapislazuli encased in gold', find-place plotted on plan. HM 839 = CMS II 3,24. Unpublished by Evans.

13–18.  *AE/NB* 1924 p.24 right, 'H. of Frescoes Intaglios found in its area', a description of six seals with three sketches (PLATE 48(h)). 1st, HM 1287 = CMS II 4,111; 2nd, HM 1282 = CMS II 4,112; 3rd, HM 1286 = CMS II 3,21; 4th and 5th (presuming '2 Vars.' means 2 variants) HM 1280 = CMS II 3,18 and HM 1284 = CMS II 3,19; 6th, HM 1288 = CMS II 3,17. All unpublished by Evans.

19.     *AE/NB* 1922–6 p.39 'NE Stairs' in subsidiary investigations, a 'steatite lentoid' with 'agrimi and lion much mixed up' with sketch (PLATE 48(i)) and comment 'decidedly LM IIIb'. Unpublished and apparently lost.

To these may be added a further instance of a likely stamp seal.

20.     *DM/DB* 23 May 1901, S. Front, 'a grooved stamp of oval shape for impressing a pattern' and sketched as having a handle and chevron pattern on the face. No such seal is included in CMS, suggesting that it has been lost.

*Annual Reports and Palace of Minos*

The information in the excavation notebooks can be supplemented with the publication of other seals not recorded in them; but with varying degrees of reliability.

One instance may be accepted as certain since it was illustrated in the annual report following its discovery.

21.    NW Treasury, a broken cushion seal with bull's head and double-axe in *BSA* 9 (1902–3) 114, fig. 70. HM 337 = CMS II 3,11.

In *PM* Evans ascribed four seals to the Little Palace, one from later tests in the building. The other three are part of a block of seals entered in the Inventory as coming from 'Houses S. of the Palace of Knossos'. The fairly early publication of two of these in *PM* I makes an error on the part of Evans less likely, especially as more than the one recorded seal, no. 10 above, might be expected to have been found in that large structure.

22.    *PM* I.670, fig. 490; HM 843 = CMS II 3,23.
23.    *PM* I.705–6, fig. 259, wrongly described as a sealing; HM 840 = CMS II 3,22.
24.    *PM* IV.216–18, fig. 167, found below the steps of the main staircase during restoration work in 1931; HM 1419 = CMS II 3,13.
25.    *PM* IV.151, fig. 116, wrongly described as a sealing; HM 845 = CMS II 2,33.

From elsewhere may be added:

26.    *PM* II.2, fig. 517 a seal there said to have been found with a hoard of bronze vases by the Stepped Portico. *DM/DB* 1923(2) pp.34–6 describes the finding of the bronzes but does not mention the seal. It is HM 1279 = CMS II 3,16.
27.    *PM* IV.595, fig. 590, said to be from the 'Lapidary's Workshop'. Not strictly a seal but a core with a roughed-out lentoid and design. Ash. Mus. 1938.1087. Further illustrated and discussed by J.G. Younger in *BSA* 74 (1979) 263 and Plates 33–4.

Finally, two other seals are illustrated with vague or no provenience:

28.    *PM* IV.1018, fig. 966, from 'N.of the Palace site'; Ash. Mus. 1938.1020 = Kenna 302.
29.    *PM* IV.588, fig. 583 and Suppl. Plate LVj, 'from near Knossos' with pottery 'mature LM II'; Ash. Mus. 1938.1058 = Kenna 315.

That these records do not represent the true state of affairs only becomes clear from the considerable number of other seals which Evans handed over to Herakleion Museum where they were entered in the Inventory to which we now turn.

### The Inventory of Herakleion Museum

There are no entries for Evans's excavations of 1900 and 1901, the earliest being a block of seals numbered 200–221, ascribed in Greek to 'Knossos A. Evans, 1902'. These are sandwiched between two entries both with the date 1901, seals from Gournia and ones from Zakro, while the latter is followed by a series from Knossos 'geom. tombs' with a date 1900, i.e. Hogarth's excavations. From this it is not quite clear whether the date refers to the date of excavation or the year in which the seals were handed in, which might, of course, be the same. In the latter case, it would imply that there was some backlog not dealt with chronologically.

Of the group 200–221, HM 200 is no. 8 above (and it *was* found in 1902), 201 is described as a seal with handle, presumably an early stamp seal, and 221 probably not a seal at all. The remaining nineteen, all previously unpublished, now appear in volumes of CMS.[3]

Failing information about where these seals were found, little can usefully be added. If the entry '1902' refers to the excavation season, this was the year in which digging was largely concentrated in the E. wing of the Palace, namely the Court of the Spout and the region south of the Queen's Megaron as far as the Corridor of the Sword Tablets and the Shrine of the Double Axes. The only two recorded finds are nos. 7 and 8 above, near the School Room. More, of course, could have been found within the area excavated and probably were. But if all nineteen belong there, it raises a severe problem in that, with the exception of no. 10 above, a seal found in the Little Palace and itself lost, no seals can be allocated to the following year, 1903, when, among other areas, Evans dug the SE House, the Royal Villa and the NE House in which some must have been found; indeed, a considerable number to judge from comparable recent excavations.

Similar problems attach to the next entry of eight sealstones, HM 838–45, all allocated, this time without a year, to 'Houses S. of the Palace of Knossos' (in Greek). At this point, no chronological sequence is perceptible in the Inventory. The two previous entries relate to seals found by Evans in the Zafer Papoura cemetery, dug in 1904, while the succeeding entry is of a seal from the British School's excavations at Praesos, i.e. 1901, and this is followed by a list of seals purchased, with the year 1909 given to them. Someone, it seems, was catching up with outstanding work and, perhaps, making mistakes if Evans correctly allotted three of them to the Little Palace, nos. 22, 23 and 25 above. However, the location given to HM 839 can be confirmed and made more precise with a date of excavation of 1908, no. 12 above. If the remaining four seals were found the same year and the ascription of them to houses S. of the Palace is right, the S. House and the SW House, both dug in 1908, are not improbable find-places for them. They are HM 838 = CMS II 3,25, HM 841 = CMS II 4,117, HM 843 = CMS II 3,23 and HM 844 which may have been lost.[4]

Greater uncertainty attaches to the next entry of three sealstones given the year 1911 without location; HM 948 = CMS II 3,91, HM 949 = CMS II 4,143 and HM 950 = CMS II 3,94. This was a year of apparent inactivity at Knossos, so the possibility cannot be excluded that they had been found earlier but handed in that year.

Then there is a considerable chronological gap until the next block of entries, ten seals HM 1279–1288, given the year 1923. That was certainly the date when HM 1279, no. 26 above, was found and in the locality ascribed to it in the Inventory. The other nine are recorded as being from the House of the Frescoes excavated that same year. Of these, six can be identified from Evans's list of sealstones from that region, nos. 13–18 above and PLATE 48(i). The remaining three, HM 1281 = CMS II 4,113, HM 1283 = CMS II 3,20 and HM 1285 = CMS II 4,114 are likely also to be correctly located and either escaped Evans's attention or were not thought by him to warrant attention: two are in poor condition.

We next come to a group of five seals with the date 1930 only, HM 1409–1414.[5] If they derive from excavations carried out that year, then they are likely to have been found in the complex of rooms at the west boundary of the W. Court, the so-called NW Acropolis Houses, since little else of significance was dug that year.

Finally, apart from gems found in the cemeteries and the Temple Tomb, there remain three later entries. The first, a talismanic seal, HM 1437 = CMS II 3,26, is recorded as coming from the House of the Altars, no doubt what became known as the House of the High Priest, which was excavated in 1931, the year to which it is allotted. The second, a defaced amydaloid of paste, HM 1539 = CMS II 4,149, and the third, a rather crude and apparently unfinished lentoid of a lion, HM 2043 = CMS II 4,141 are merely ascribed to Evans, someone clearing out their bottom drawer, it would seem.

This somewhat lengthy and detailed examination of the evidence has, unfortunately, contributed little of significance towards determining the find-places of the latest seals. It has, however, shown that many more sealstones were discovered in the course of the excavations than is apparent from Evans's publications.

It would seem that, having apparently assumed responsibility for recording the seals found during the excavations, Evans failed to carry out this undertaking at all adequately. No doubt, some of his records and notes have been lost, but had they contained the same amount of information with sketches as exist for the sealings, he would surely have used these, particularly for PM IV where he discussed seals, their shapes, chronology and iconography in considerable detail. Some of the unpublished seals would have provided good examples of various aspects which concerned him, for example HM 206 (CMS II 3,88) with its suckling scene, HM 207 (CMS II 3,92) a stylized octopus, and for his discussion of 'swine' in PM IV.572, HM 1286 (CMS II 3,21). Even more unaccountable is his forgetfulness of the outstanding gold-mounted lentoid of lapis lazuli with its engraving of Master and lion, no. 12 above.

Although he, assuredly, gave priority to the tablets and their recording, followed, perhaps, by the frescoes, it might be expected that sealstones would have come soon after in claiming his attention, given his life-long concern with them. As it is, of the 28 or so recorded as having been found and the further 46 unrecorded except for their registration in Herakleion Museum, only thirteen were published by him. To these may be added a probable thirteen other seals subsequently discovered among the excavation finds in the Stratigraphical Museum at Knossos, all admittedly too worn to have deserved at that time his attention.[6]

It seems that, as with the sealings, when preparing his publications in subsequent years, he relied heavily on his early notes and the drawings which he commissioned to be made at the time. Once the material had been handed over to Herakleion Museum, it apparently remained there without further study, and, often, forgotten.

## NOTES

1. It must be stressed that there could well be other records which a more detailed examination of the Evans Archive might uncover.
2. See note 13 above to Section 1.
3. HM 200 = CMS II 3,8; HM 201 = CMS II 2,30; HM202 = CMS II 3,89; HM203 = CMS II 3,90; HM 204 = CMS II 3,93; HM205 = CMS II 4,138; HM 206 = CMS II 3,88; HM207 = CMS II 3,92; HM 208 = CMS II, 4,146; HM 209 = CMS II 4,13; HM 211 = CMS II 4,145; HM 212 = CMS II 4,11; HM 213 = CMS II 3,86; HM 214 = CMS II 4,9; HM 215 = CMS II 4,15; HM 216 = CMS II 4,140; HM 217 = CMS II 3,95; HM 218 = CMS II 3,97; HM 219 = CMS II 4,14; HM 220 = CMS II 4,137.
4. HM 844 is described in the Inventory as being a flattened cylinder engraved with a standing woman having her right hand on her hip and her left upraised; in front of her two ?female dresses. It does not appear in CMS, and, so, may be lost.
5. HM 1409 = CMS II 4,139; HM 1410 = CMS II 3,87; HM 1411 = CMS II 4,136; HM 1412 = CMS II 4,142; HM 1413 = CMS II 2,41; HM 1414 = CMS II 4,147.
6. Published by J. Betts in *BSA* 62 (1969) 27f. and by J. Younger and J. Betts in *BSA* 74 (1979) 270f.

# PLATES

Scale:

Photographs    *c.*5:2
Drawings    *c.*2:1
Notebooks    lifesize or slightly smaller

PLATE 1

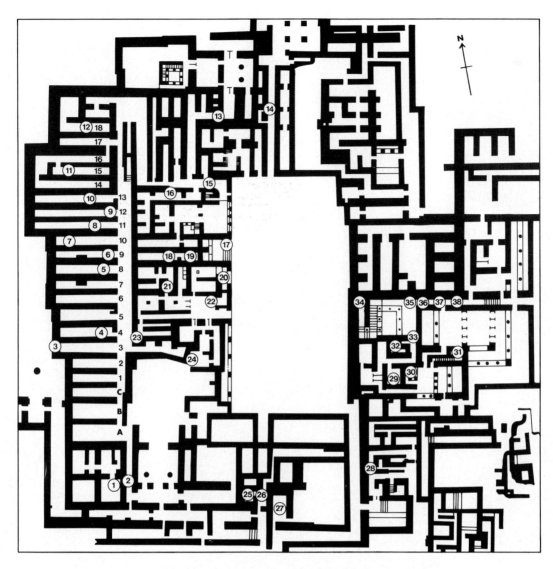

Plan of the Palace at Knossos showing distribution of latest sealings

F.  1. South West Door
    2. Corridor of the Cupbearer Fresco

G.  3. Magazine 3
    4. Magazine 4
    5. Magazine 8
    6. Magazine 9
    7. Magazine 10
    8. Magazine 11
    9. Magazine 12
   10. Magazine 13
   11. Magazine 15
   12. Magazine 18

J.  13. North of the Room of the Stirrup Jars
   14. North Entrance Passage

O.  15. Corridor of the Stone Basin
   16. Threshold between Rooms of the Stone Bench and
       the Stone Drum
   17. Stepped Portico

K.  18. Room of the Jewel Fresco
   19. Room of the Warrior Seal

M.  20. Central Shrine

O.  21. Room of the Niche
   22. Room of the Column Bases
   23. Corridor of the House Tablets
   24. Room of the Chariot Tablets
   25. Room of the Seal Impressions
   26. Room of the Clay Signet
   27. Room of the Egyptian Beans

S.  28. Corridor of the Sword Tablets

R.  29. Treasury Room
   30. Bathroom of the Queen's Megaron
   31. Secret Staircase
   32. Wooden Staircase (Corridor of the Demon Seals)
   33. Doorway South of the Hall of the Colonnades
   34. Landing of the Grand Staircase
   35. Doorway North of the Hall of the Colonnades
   36. Upper East-West Corridor
   37. Lower East-West Corridor
   38. Top of the East-West Staircase

PLATE 2

F1
123

F2
( 258/2 )

G3
240

1023

G5

241

239

G6
1938. 1080

G7
137

G11
113

G8
136

G9
376
1-2

G10
209

Sealings with provenance. (F) SW Corner; (G) W. Magazines

PLATE 3

G12
165

G13
284

G15
1938.861

G14
285

J1
129

1938, 1016

J3
146

J2
109

K1
1938.981

K2
114

K2
K11

168
1–2

Sealings with provenance. (G) W. Magazines; (J) Northern Quarter; (K) Area of the Jewel Fresco

PLATE 4

K2
115

K3
164

K5
297

K4  K12
Q21

1938. 1014 b

214

215

258/1

K6
295

K8
167

K7
299

K9
298

K10
296

K13
1219

K16
362

Sealings with provenance. (K) Area of the Jewel Fresco

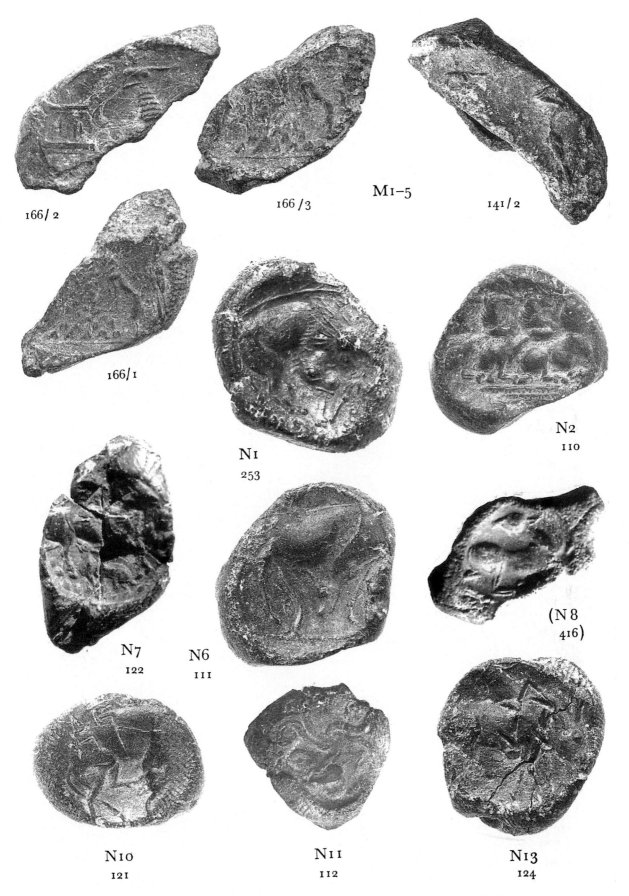

PLATE 5

166/2  166/3  M1–5  141/2

166/1  N1 253  N2 110

N7 122  N6 111  (N8 416)

N10 121  N11 112  N13 124

Sealings with provenance. (M) The Central Shrine; (N) The Room of the Chariot Tablets

PLATE 6

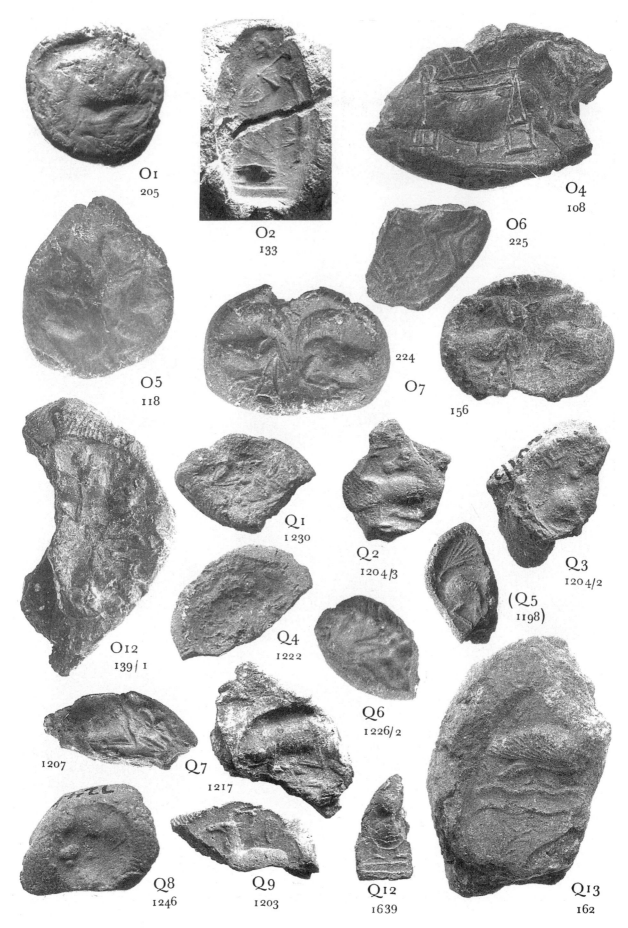

O1
205

O2
133

O4
108

O6
225

O5
118

224

O7
156

Q1
1230

Q2
1204/3

Q3
1204/2

(Q5
1198)

O12
139/1

Q4
1222

Q6
1226/2

1207

Q7
1217

Q8
1246

Q9
1203

Q12
1639

Q13
162

Sealings with provenance. (O) W. Wing, various; (Q) SW Basements

PLATE 7

134

135

Q14

Q15
1209

Q16
360

Q17
1938, 1047

Q18
1303

Q19

161    160

Q20
143

Q22
283

{ R1
{ R51
{ R54

1938. 1015 a

278

Sealings with provenance. (Q) SW Basements; (R) Domestic Quarter

PLATE 8

R1
R51
R54

279

277

R2
148

R3
289

R4
293

R6

1000

1005

213

212

R7
208

R8
250

R9
251

R10
221

Sealings with provenance. Domestic Quarter, R1 Upper E-W Corridor, R2–10 Landing of Grand Staircase

PLATE 9

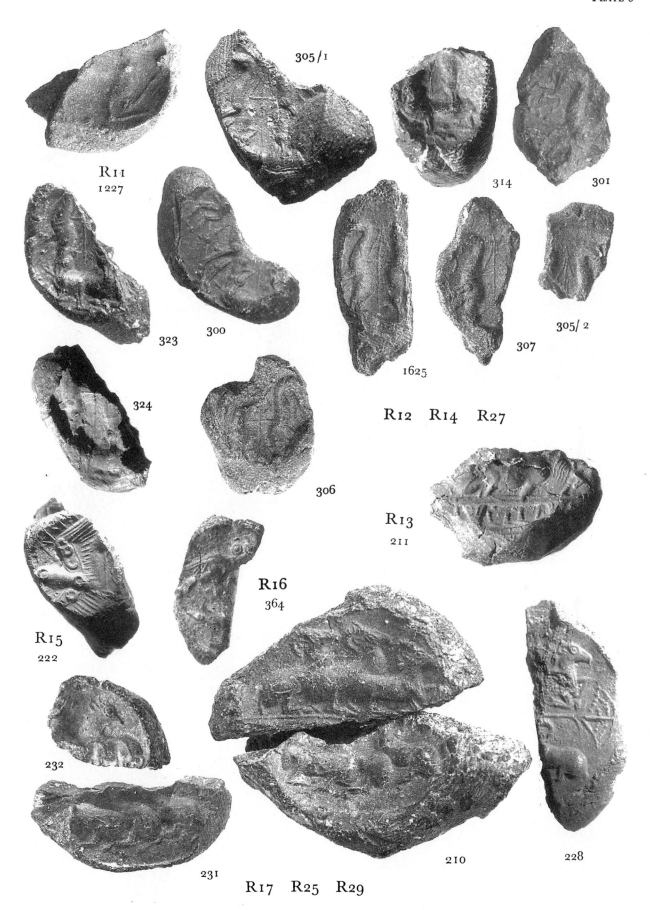

R11
1227

305/1

314

301

323

300

1625

307

305/2

324

306

R12   R14   R27

R13
211

R16
364

R15
222

232

R17   R25   R29

231

210

228

Sealings with provenance. (R) Domestic Quarter, Landing of Grand Staircase

PLATE 10

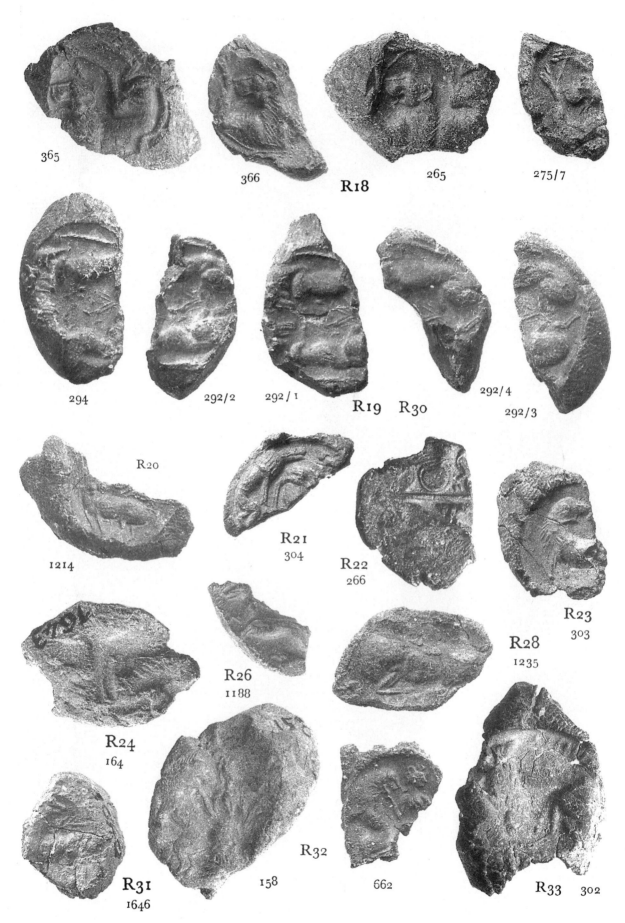

365

366

R18    265    275/7

294    292/2    292/1    R19    R30    292/4    292/3

R20    R21    R22    R23
1214    304    266    303

R24    R26    R28
164    1188    1235

R31    R32    R33
1646    158    662    302

Sealings with provenance. (R) Domestic Quarter, Landing of Grand Staircase

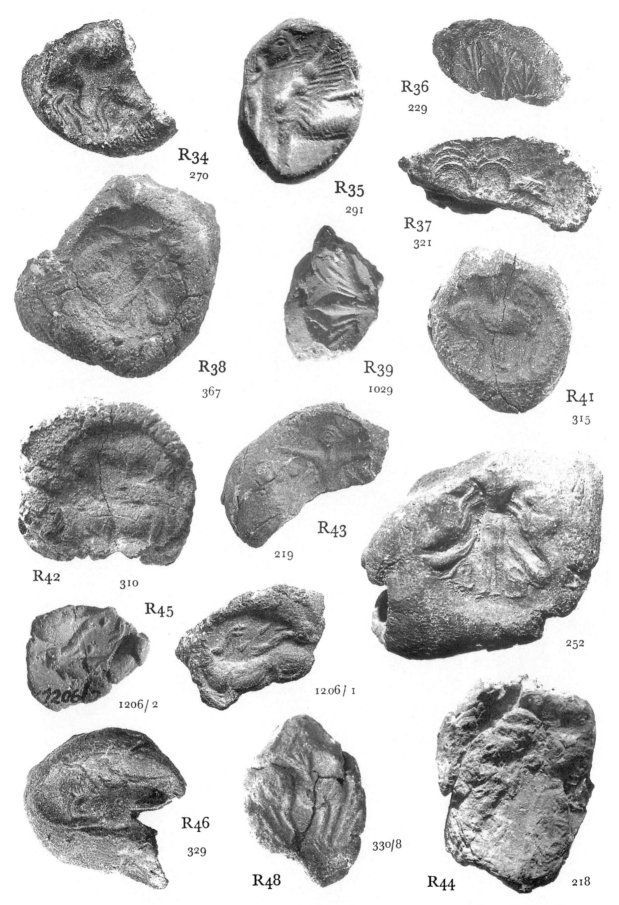

Plate 11

R36
229

R34
270

R35
291

R37
321

R38
367

R39
1029

R41
315

R42          310

R43
219

R45
1206/2

12.06/1

252

R46
329

R48

330/8

R44          218

Sealings with provenance. (R) Domestic Quarter, R34–37 Landing of Grand Staircase, R38–48 Lower E-W Corridor

PLATE 12

317     318     R49

316

243     245     R50

R52     330/1     1247

268

274     242     244

R57     1302

R60     260     361

R61     267     R63     271     R66     272     R70     1238

R67     1197/1-2     R69     287     R71     1229     311/7

Sealings with provenance. Domestic Quarter, R49–52 Lower E-W Corridor, R53–66 doorway S. of Hall of Colonnades and beyond, R67–71 Wooden Staircase

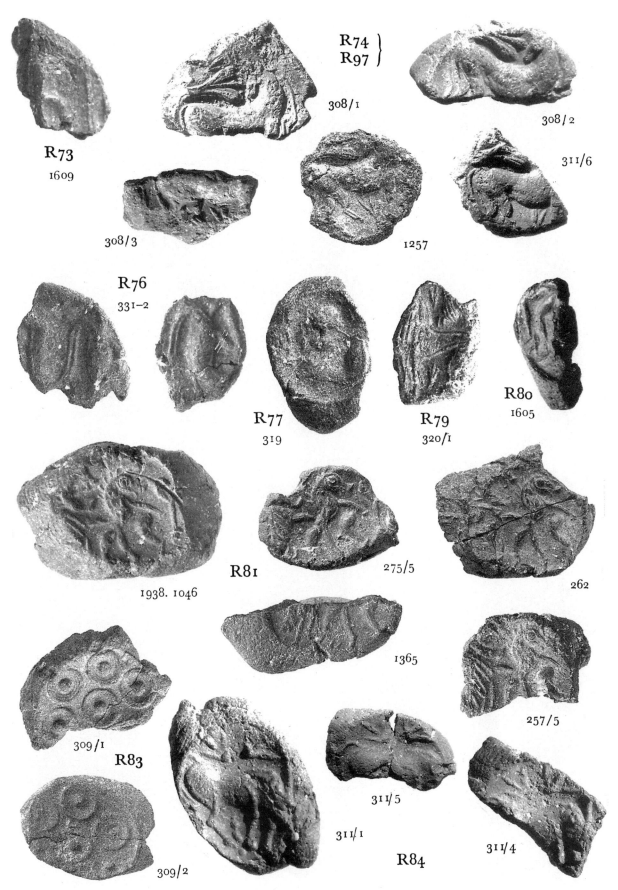

PLATE 13

R74
R97 }

308/1

308/2

311/6

R73
1609

308/3

1257

R76
331-2

R77
319

R79
320/1

R80
1605

1938. 1046

R81

275/5

262

1365

257/5

309/1

R83

309/2

311/5

311/1

R84

311/4

Sealings with provenance. (R) Domestic Quarter, Wooden Staircase

PLATE 14

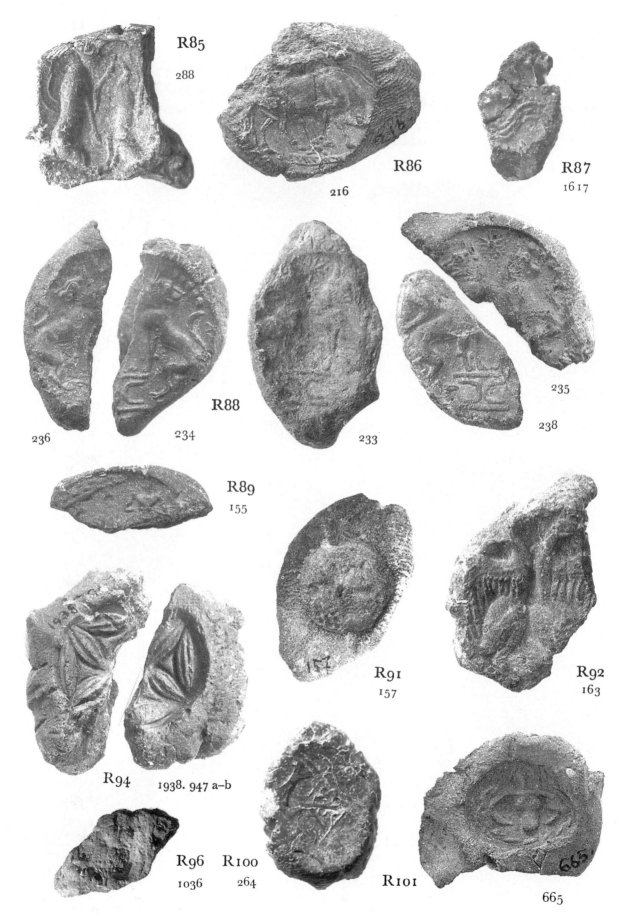

R85
288

R86
216

R87
1617

R88
236    234

233

235

238

R89
155

R94    1938. 947 a–b

R91
157

R92
163

R96    R100
1036    264

R101

665

Sealings with provenance. Domestic Quarter, R86–7 Wooden Staircase, R88–99 Wooden Stairs and Secretaries 'Bureau', R100–1 Room of Stone Bench

PLATE 15

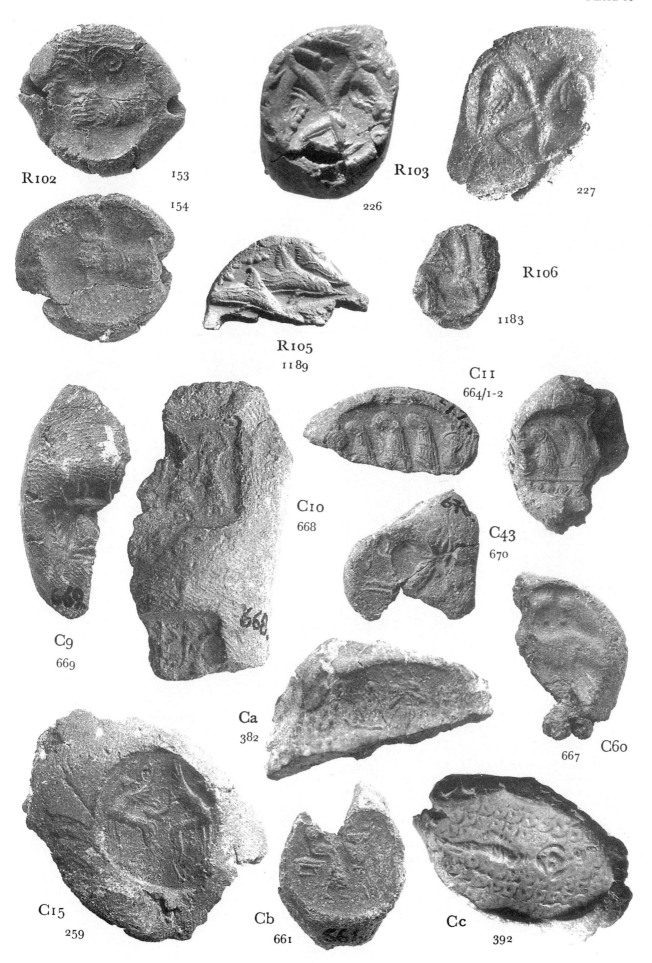

R102　153

154

R103　226

227

R106　1183

R105　1189

C11　664/1-2

C10　668

C43　670

C9　669

Ca　382

C60　667

C15　259

Cb　661

Cc　392

Sealings with provenance. Domestic Quarter, R102–6 Queen's Megaron, C11–Cc ascribed to Domestic Quarter

PLATE 16

S1

U2
421

U7
424

U12
423

U19
422

U31
651

U56
418

U66
658

U107
419

U104
652

U106
654

U114
663

U115
656

U54
U117
659

U112
417

Vb
375

Va

Ox. 1938. 1068

Vc
403

Vd
400/3

Sealings with provenance. S1 Corridor of the Sword Tablets; (U) Little Palace; Va-Vd Arsenal

PLATE 17

G3-4
1542

O12
139/2

Q2-3
1204/1

Q6
1226/1

(Q17)
1092

R1
R51
R54

280

281

282

R12
1237

R19
1234

R29
210/2

R43
220

R46

1208

275/2

275/6

R81

273

257/2

Sealings with provenance. Additional examples from various areas

PLATE 18

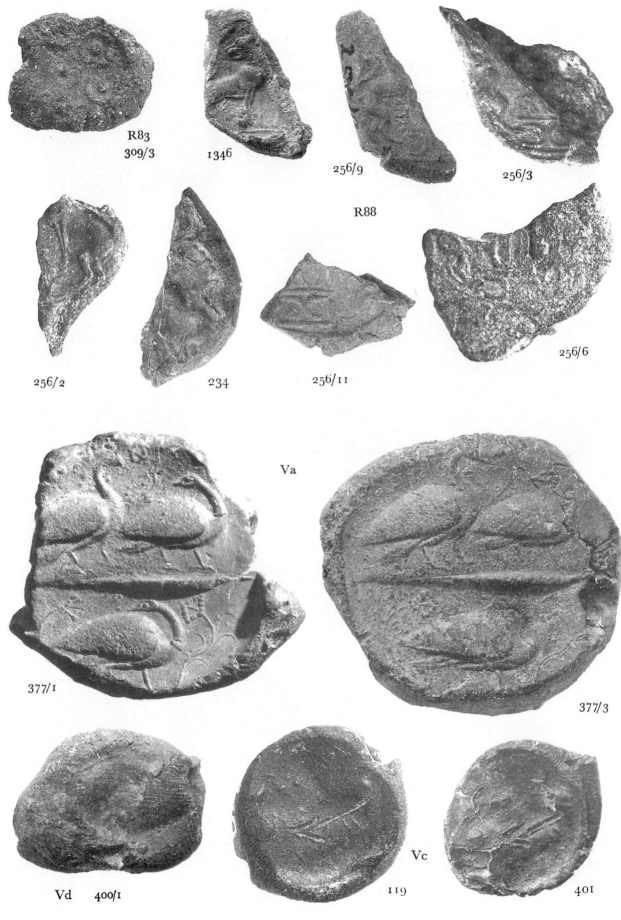

R83
309/3

1346

256/9

256/3

R88

256/2

234

256/11

256/6

Va

377/1

377/3

Vd    400/1

119

Vc

401

Sealings with provenance. Additional examples from various areas

PLATE 19

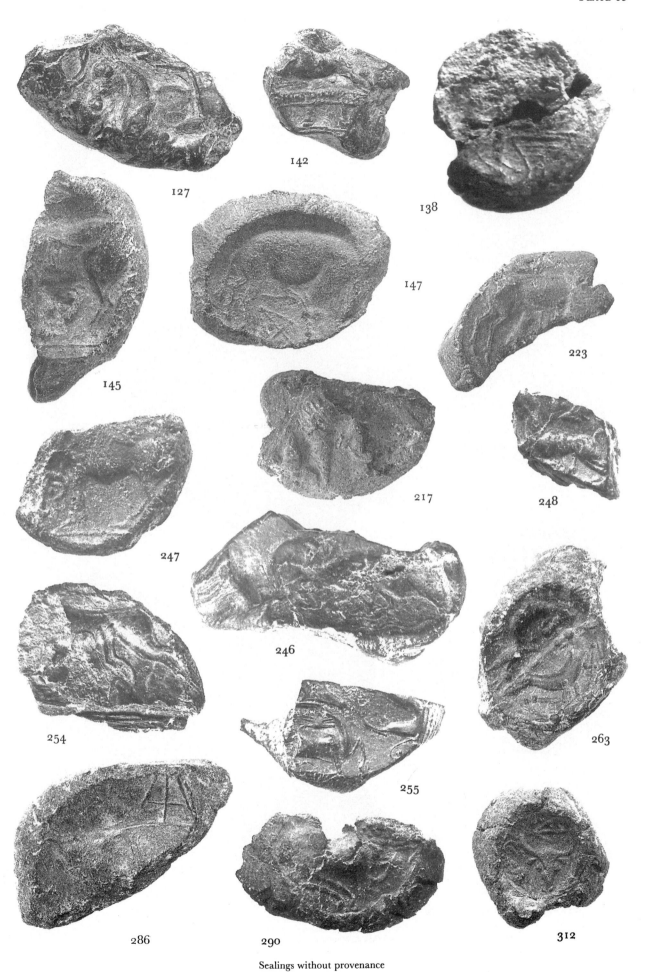

142

127

138

145

147

223

247

217

248

246

254

263

255

286

290

312

Sealings without provenance

PLATE 20

313

325 / 1-2

326 / 1-2

328

327

378

369
Ec

370

381

380

379

( 414 bought )

650

653

Sealings without provenance. HMs 369 possibly erroneously ascribed to Little Palace (Ec)

PLATE 21

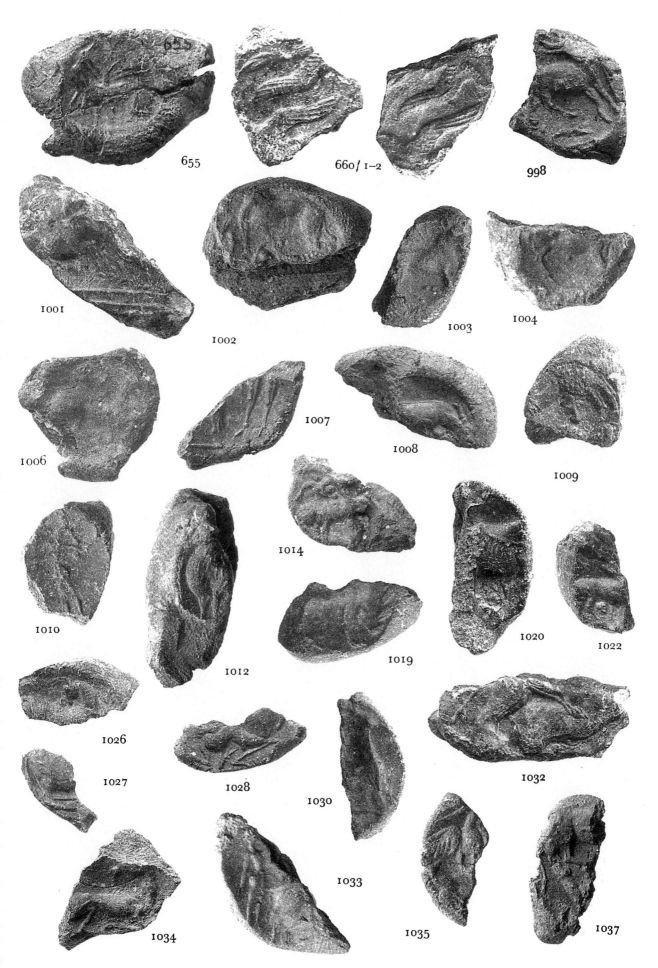

655

660/1–2

998

1001

1002

1003

1004

1006

1007

1008

1009

1010

1012

1014

1019

1020

1022

1026

1027

1028

1030

1032

1033

1034

1035

1037

Sealings without provenance

PLATE 22

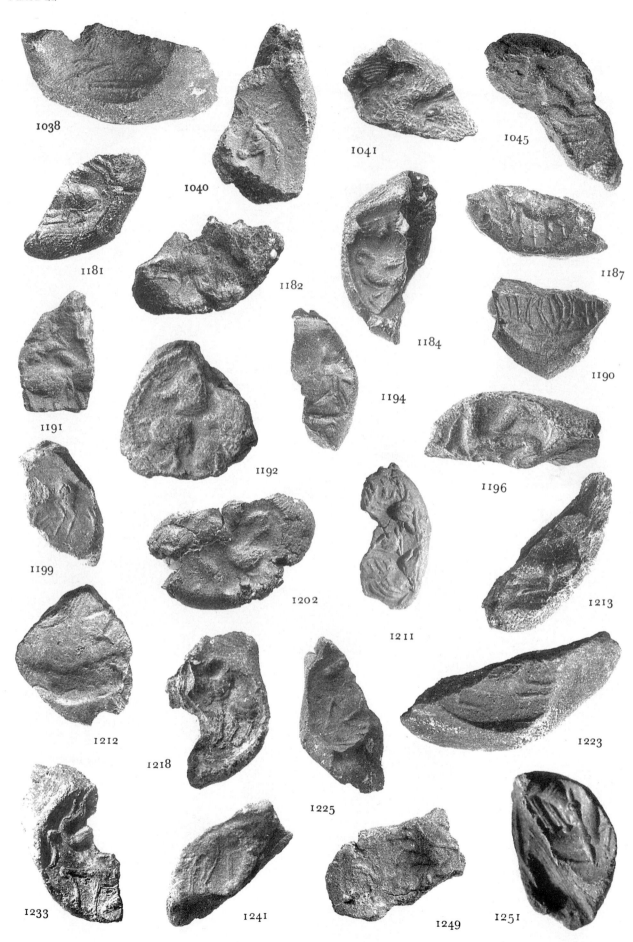

1038

1040

1041

1045

1181

1182

1184

1187

1190

1191

1192

1194

1196

1199

1202

1211

1213

1212

1218

1223

1225

1233

1241

1249

1251

Sealings without provenance

PLATE 23

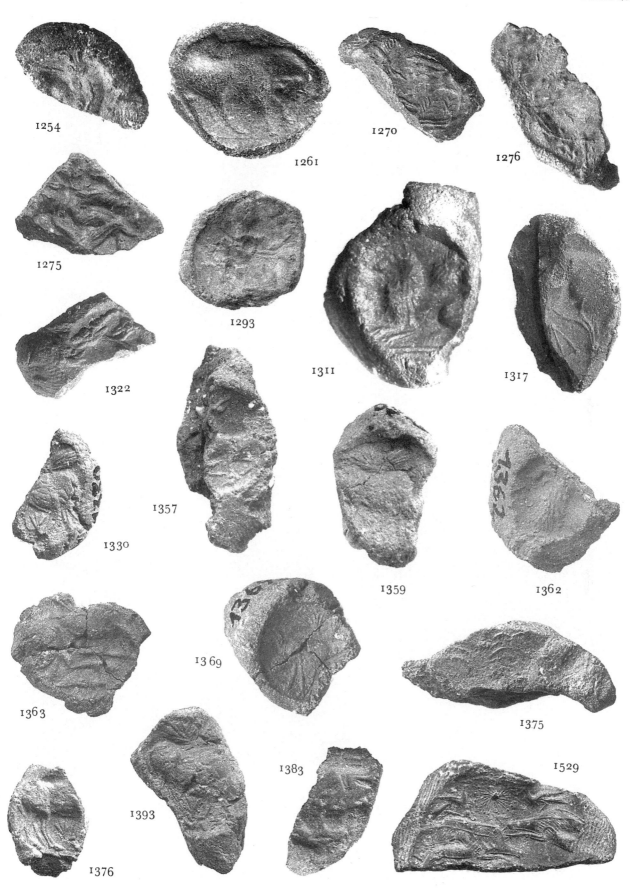

1254

1261

1270

1276

1275

1293

1311

1317

1322

1330

1357

1359

1362

1363

1369

1375

1529

1376

1393

1383

Sealings without provenance

PLATE 24

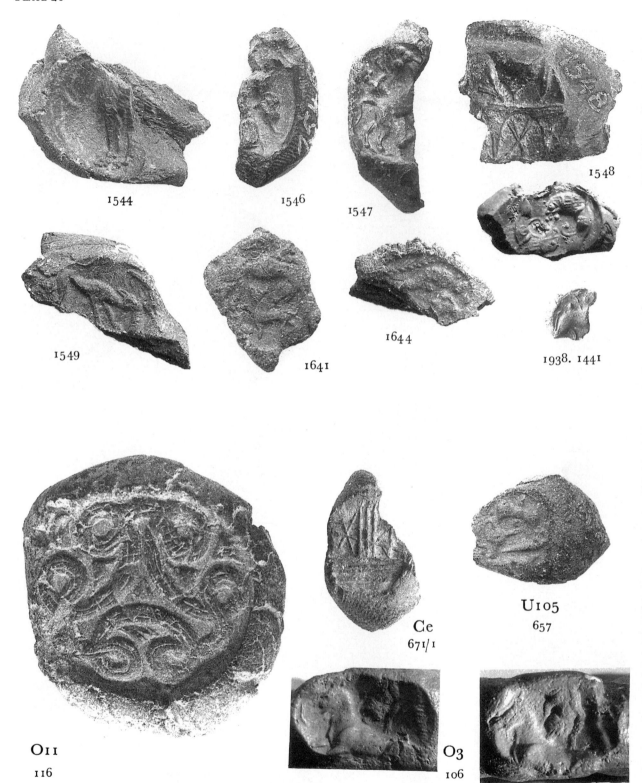

1544

1546

1547

1548

1549

1641

1644

1938. 1441

O11

116

Ce
671/1

U105
657

O3
106

(top) sealings without provenance; (below) sealings from early seals probably out of context

PLATE 25

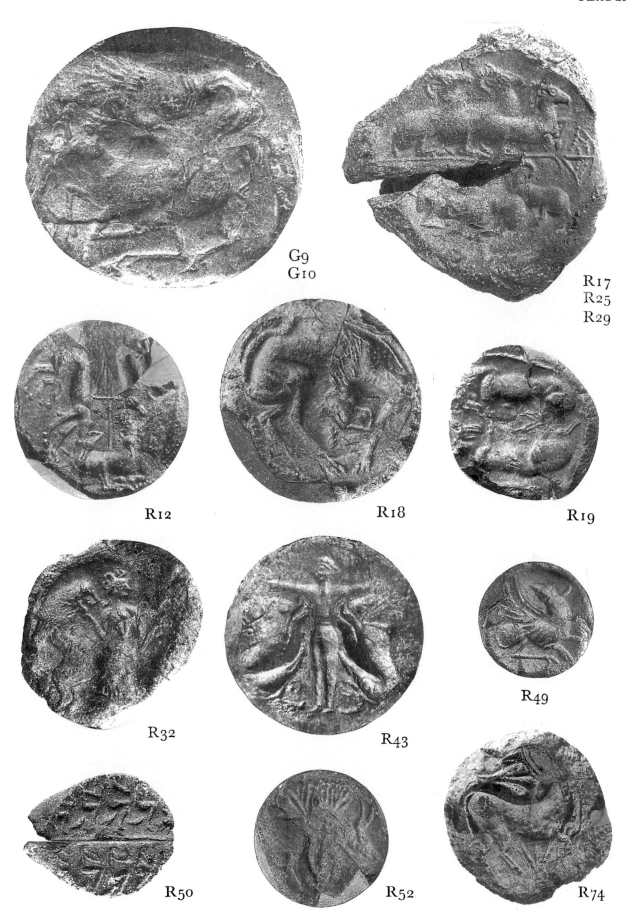

G9
G10

R17
R25
R29

R12

R18

R19

R32

R43

R49

R50

R52

R74

Reconstructions by photographic montage of multiple sealings. G9–10 Magazine 11: (R) from E. Wing

PLATE 26

R81

R83

R88

R94

R103

C11

328
1008

370
381

255
1529

660 i-2

Reconstructions by photographic montage of multiple sealings. (R) and C11 from Domestic Quarter; remainder without provenance

PLATE 27

G3

G6

G8

G11

G10

G15

J2

J3

K1

K2

K4  K12
Q21

M1–5

K16

N7

N10

N13

O2

Drawings of sealings. G3 Betts 17; G6 = *SM* I 43 fig.20b, *PM* III 231 fig.163, IV 617 fig.604b; G8 = *PM* IV 626 fig.613; G10 = *PM* IV 535 fig.486; G11 = *PM* IV 535 fig.487; G15 = *PM* IV 736 fig.721; J2 = *PM* IV 568 fig.542a; J3 = *PM* II 244 fig.141b, IV 827 fig.806; K1 = *PM* I 716 fig.539b; K2 = *PM* IV 602 fig.596; K4, K12 and Q21 = *PM* II 765 fig.493, IV 581 fig.567 and 609 fig.597B(j); K16 AE not published; M1–5 *BSA* 7 (1900–1) 29 fig.9, PM II 809 fig.528, III 463 fig.323, IV 608 fig.597A(e); N7 Kenna fig. 1; N10 Kenna fig.5; N13 Kenna fig.2; O2 = *PM* IV 414 fig.343b

PLATE 28

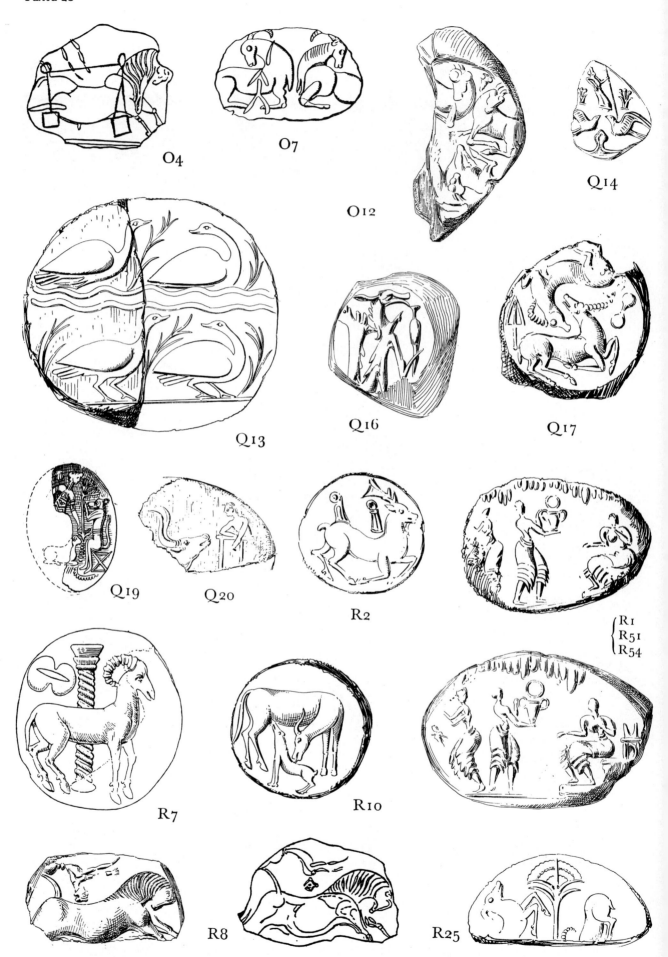

O4    O7    O12    Q14

Q13    Q16    Q17

Q19    Q20    R2    {R1 / R51 / R54

R7    R10

R8    R25

Drawings of sealings. O4 Betts *Kadmos* 6(1967) 39 fig.11; O7 Kenna fig.4; O12 = *PM* IV 609 fig.597B(c); Q13 = *PM* IV 609 fig.597B(e); Q14 = *PM* II 766 fig.497, IV 609 fig.597B(i); Q16 AE not published; Q17 = *PM* IV 570 fig.544c; Q19 = *BSA* 7 (1900–1) 18 fig.7a, *PM* II 763 fig.491, IV 387 fig.321; Q20 = *PM* IV 564 fig.532; R1, 51, 54 = *PM* II 767 fig.498, IV 395 fig.331 and 597 fig.591; R2 = *PM* IV 577 fig.562 and 609 fig.597B(1); R7 = *PM* III 317 fig.208; R8(left) = *BSA* 8 (1901–2) 78 fig.43, *PM* I 686 fig.504d, III 219 fig.153,(right) Betts *Kadmos* 6(1967) 39 fig.11; R10 = *PM* IV 609 fig.597B(d); R25 AE not published

PLATE 29

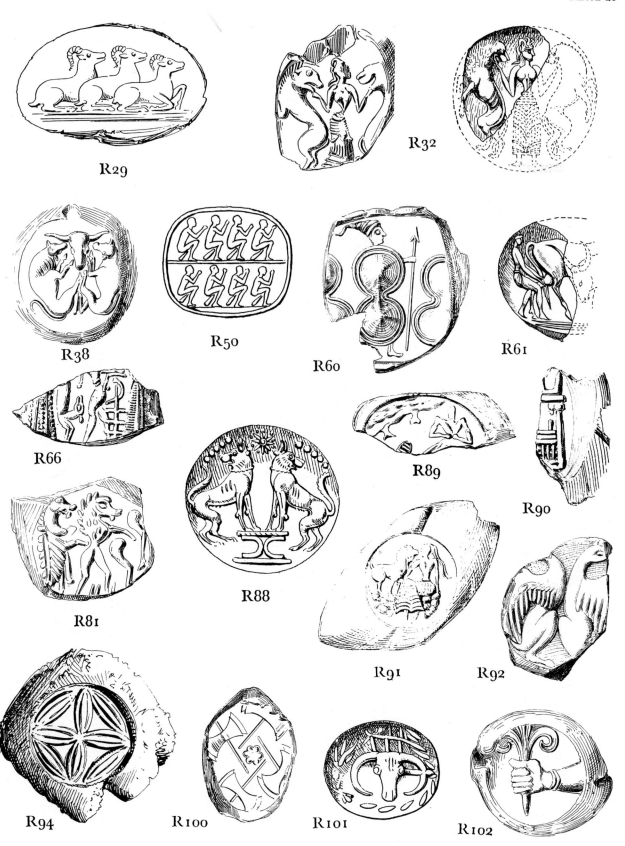

Drawings of sealings. R29 = *PM* IV 609 fig.597B(f); R32(left) HMs 158 = *PM* IV 608 fig.597A(c), (right) HMs 662 = *PM* IV 608 fig.597A(a); R38 = *PM* IV 609 fig.597B(g); R50 = *PM* IV 521 fig.463; R60 = *BSA* 8 (1901–2) 77 fig.41, *PM* III 313, fig.205; R61 = *PM* IV 564 fig.534; R66 = *BSA* 8 (1901–2) 77 fig.40, *PM* IV 598 fig.593; R81 = *PM* IV 441 fig.365; R88 = *PM* IV 608 fig.597A(g); R89,90 and 91 AE not published; R92 = *PM* I 712 fig.536c; R94 = *PM* IV 626 fig.616; R100 = *BSA* 8 (1901–2) 103 fig.61, *PM* IV 608 fig.597A(d); R101 = *PM* IV 609 fig.597B(h); R102 = *BSA* 8 (1901–2) 78 fig.42, *PM* IV 608 fig.597A(f)

PLATE 30

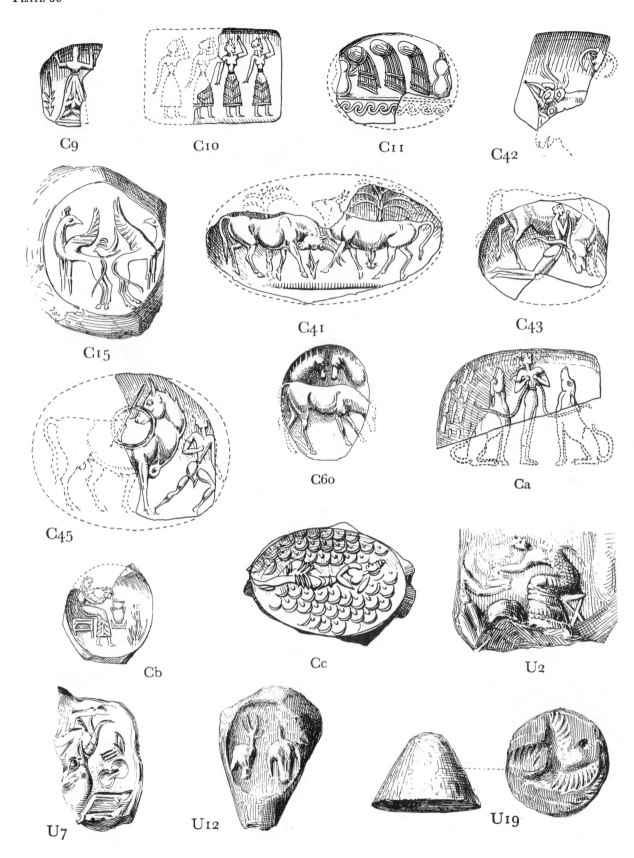

C9    C10    C11    C42

C15    C41    C43

C45    C60    Ca

Cb    Cc    U2

U7    U12    U19

Drawings of sealings. C9 AE not published; C10 = *PM* IV 608 fig.597A(b); C11 = *PM* IV 608 fig.597A(k); C15 = *PM* IV 608 fig.597A(1); C41 = *PM* IV 609 fig.597B(m); C42 = *PM* IV 608 fig.597B(n); C43 = *PM* IV 609 fig.597B(k); C45 = *PM* IV 564 fig.533; C60 AE not published; Ca = *PM* II 765 fig.495, IV 581 fig.566; Cb = *PM* IV 451 fig.367b, *JHS* 45 (1925) 18 fig.20; Cc = *PM* IV 956 fig.925; U2 = *PM* IV 387 fig.322; U7 = *PM* IV 609 597B(a); U12 and U19 AE not published

PLATE 31

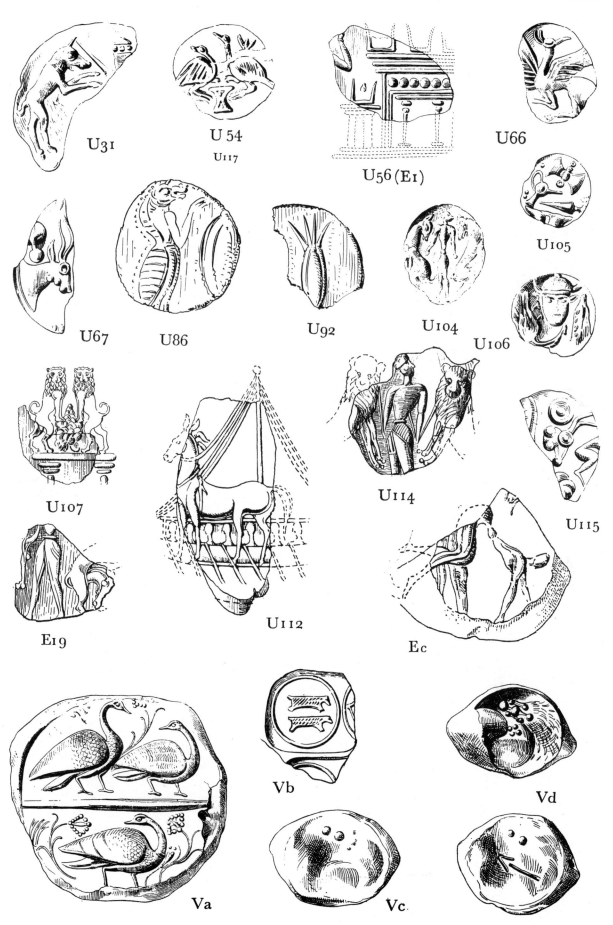

U31

U 54
U117

U 56 (E1)

U66

U67    U86

U92

U104

U106

U105

U107

E19

U112

U114

U115

Ec

Va

Vb

Vd

Vc

Drawings of sealings. U31 and 54 AE not published; U56 = *BSA* 11 (1904–5) 12 fig.5, *PM* II 524 fig.326, IV 608 fig.597A(j); U66 and 67 AE not published; U86 *PM* IV 626 fig.614; U92 = *PM* IV 626 fig.615; U 104 and 106 AE not published; U107 = *BSA* 11 (1904–5) 12 fig.6, *PM* II 524 fig.327, IV 608 fig.597A(i); U112 = *BSA* 11 (1904–5) 13 fig.7, *PM* II 244 fig.141a, IV 827 fig.805; U114 = *PM* IV 608 fig.597A(h); E19 = *PM* IV 609 fig.597B(b); Ec = *PM* IV 600 fig.594; Va = *BSA* 10 (1903–4) 56 fig.19, *PM* III 117 fig.67, IV 615 fig.602; Vb = *BSA* 10 (1903–4) 57 fig.20; Vc and d = *BSA* X(1903–4) 60 fig.22, *PM* IV fig.603

PLATE 32

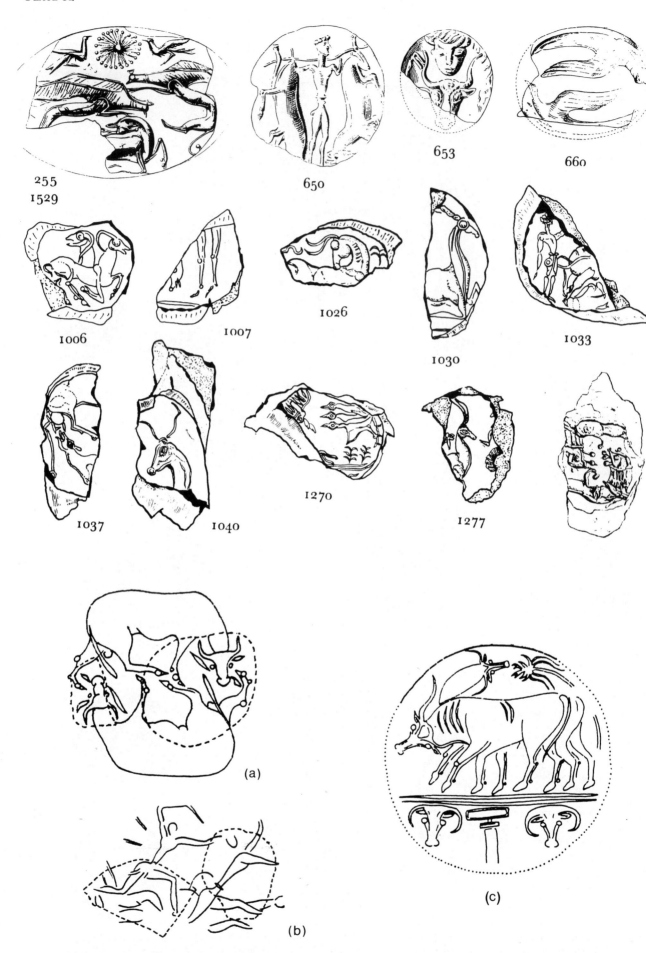

Drawings of sealings without provenance. HMs 255 + 1529 Pini, *Philia Epi* Pl.52; HMs 650,653 and 660 AE not published; HMs 1006 Betts 43; HMs 1007 Betts 47; HMs 1026 Betts 32; HMs 1030 Betts 29; HMs 1033 Betts 10; HMs 1037 Betts 13; HMs 1040 Betts 3; HMs 1270 Betts 16; HMs 1277 Betts 23; unnumbered, Betts *BSA* 74(1979)274 no.9 and Pls.39–40. (a–c) Composite diagrams by M.Gill. (a) (G3) HMs 240 and 1023; (b) HMS 1275 and 369; (c) (J2) HMs 109 and Athens NM 5405a

PLATE 33

Extracts from Evans's Note-Books. F1 1900,24; F2 1900,27; G3 and 5 1900,70; G6 1900,50 bis; G7 1901,1 bis; G8 1901,6

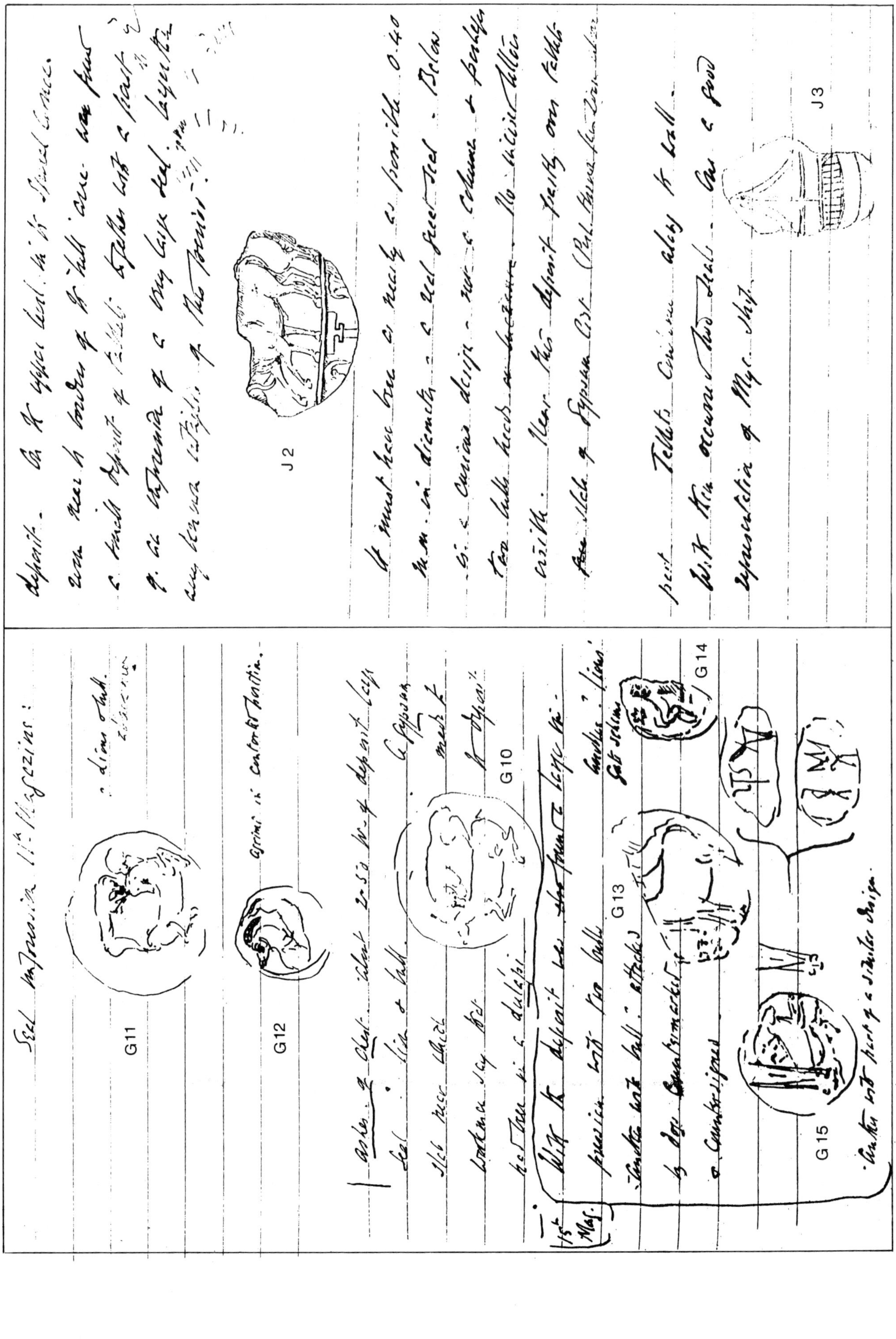


Extracts from Evans's Note-Books. G11–12 1901,7; G10–15 1901,6 bis; J2 1900,69; J3 1900,72

PLATE 35

Extracts from Evans's Note-Books. K1–4 1901,17; K5–9 1901,28 bis; K10 1901,29; K13–16 1901,26

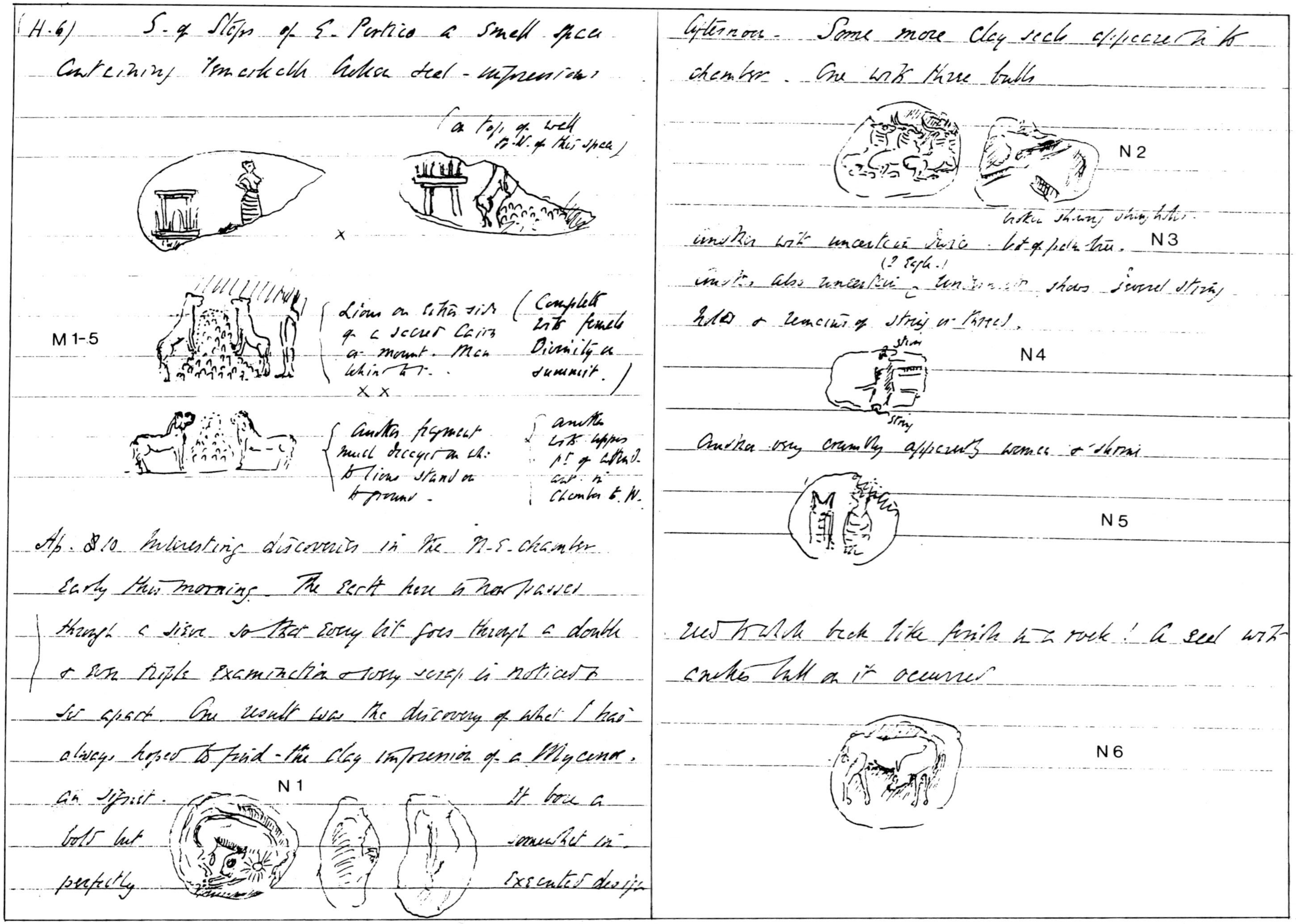

PLATE 36

N2

N3

N4

N5

N6

M1-5

N1

PLATE 37

PLATE 38

PLATE 39

Q8

Q9

Q10

Q11

Q12

Q13

Q14

Q15

Q16

Q17

Q18

Q19

Q20

Q21

Extracts from Evans's Note-Books. Q8–16 1901,16bis; Q17–18 1901,17; Q19–20 1901,33 bis

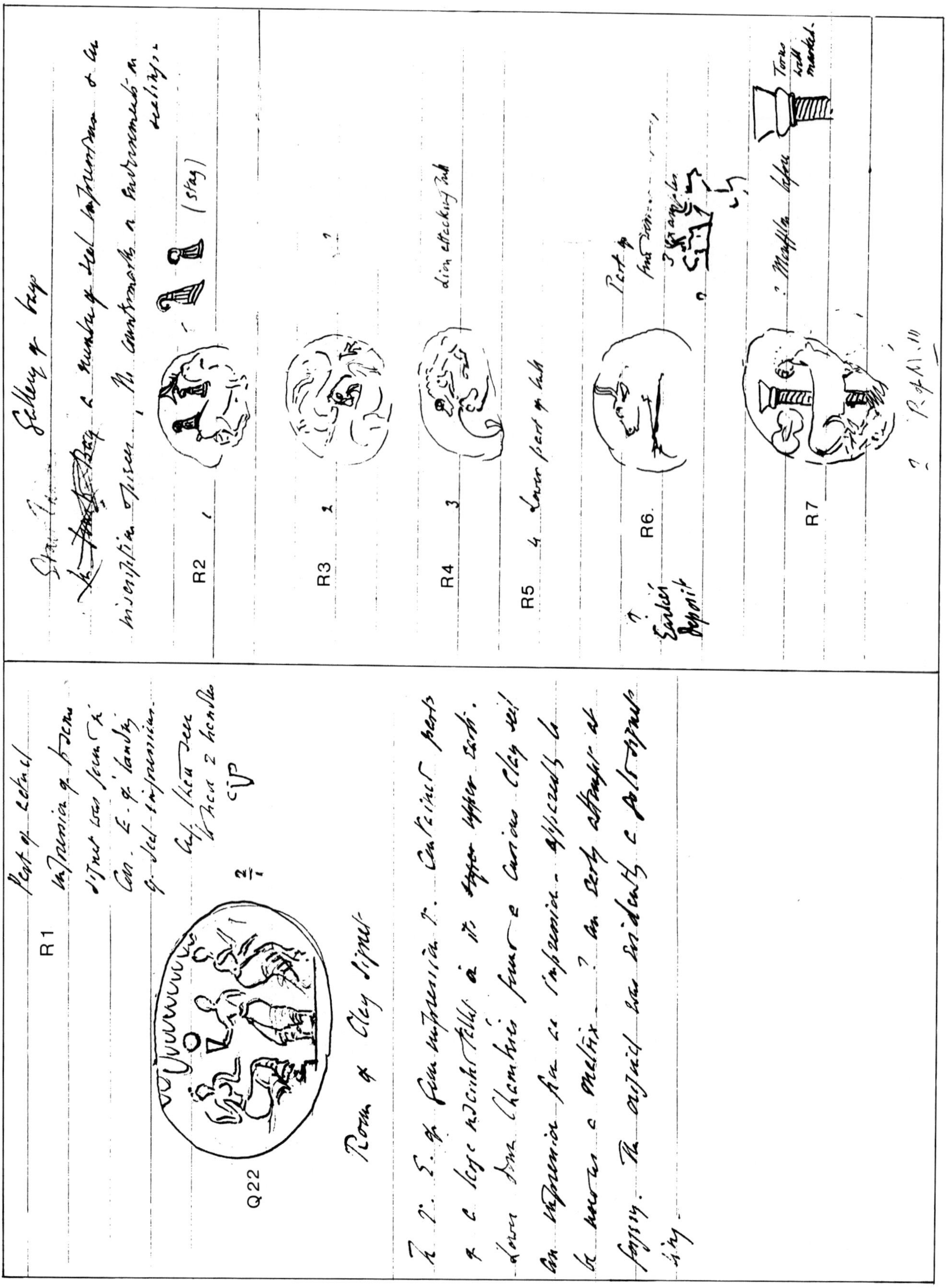

PLATE 40

R1

Q22

R2

R3

R4

R5

R6.

R7

Extracts from Evans's Note-Books. Q22 1901,34; R2–7 1901,46

PLATE 41

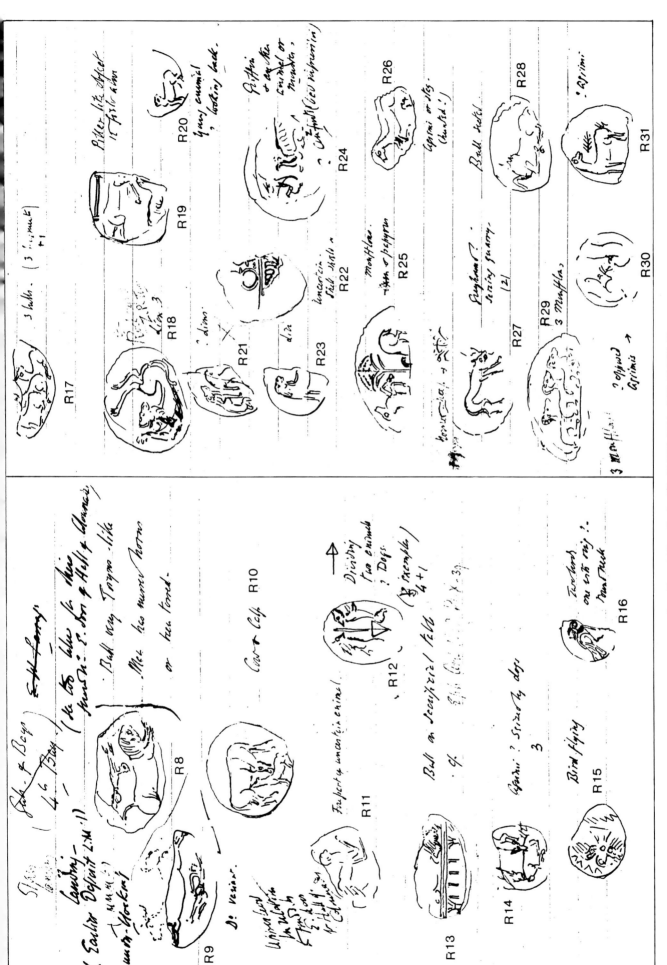

PLATE 42

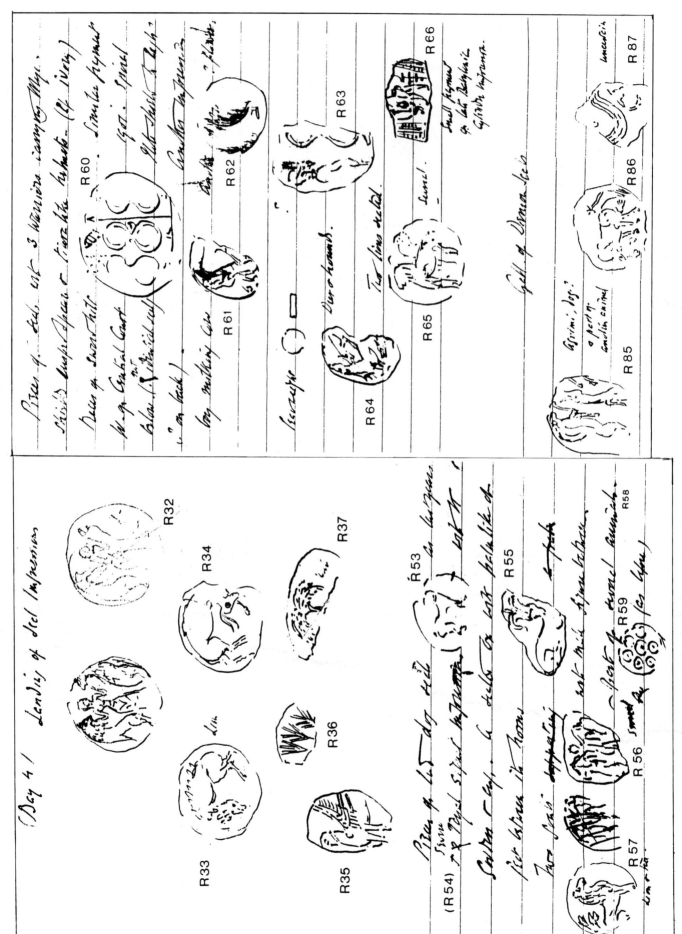

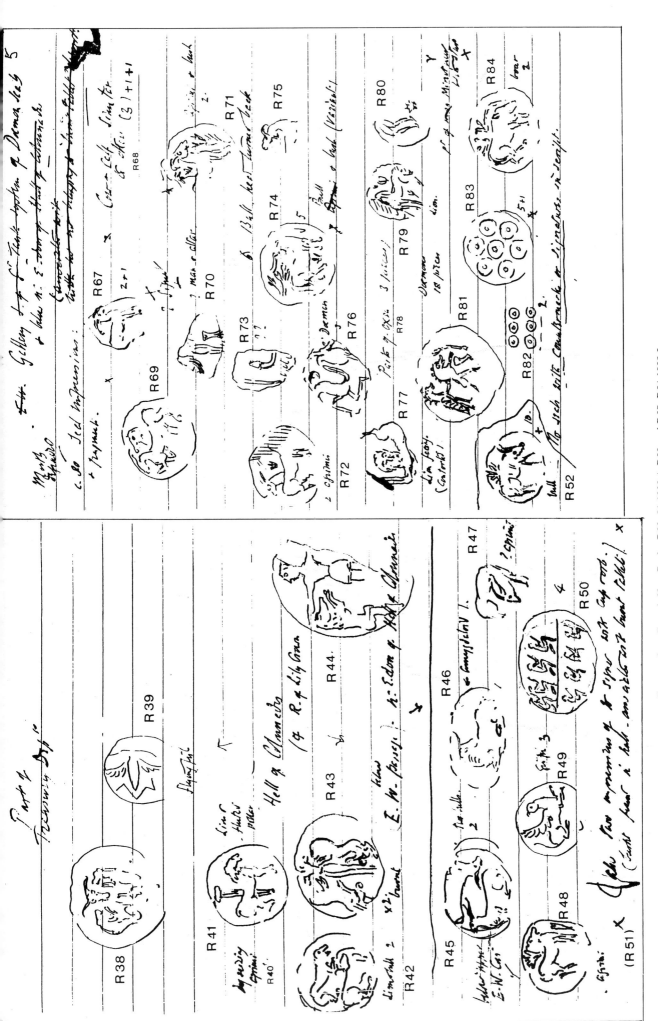

PLATE 43

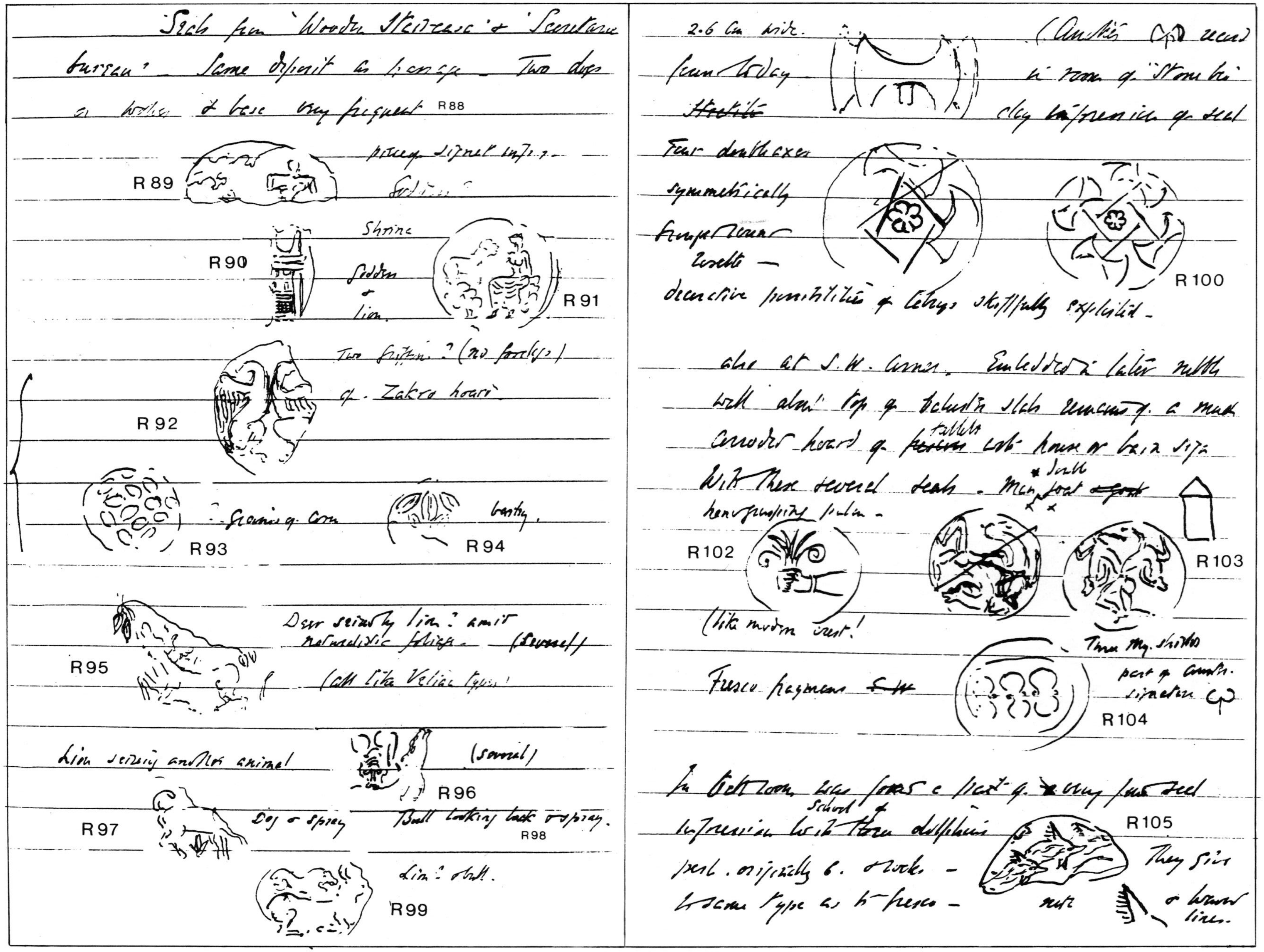

PLATE 44

R88
R89
R90
R91
R92
R93
R94
R95
R96
R97
R98
R99
R100
R102
R103
R104
R105

PLATE 45

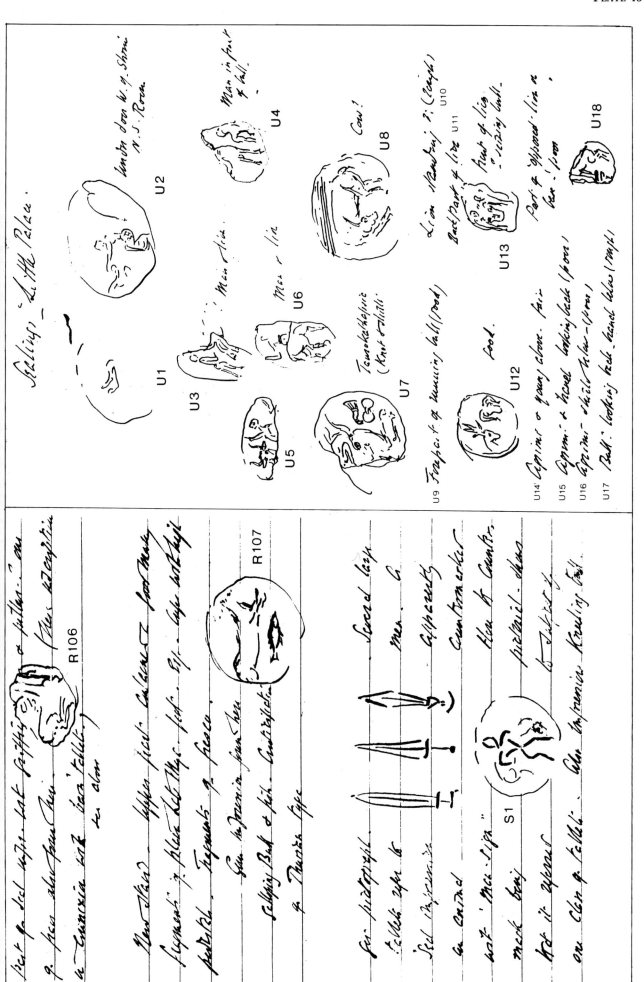

Extracts from Evans's Note-Books. R106 1902,43; R107 1902,45; S1 1902,34; U1–18 1905,9

PLATE 46

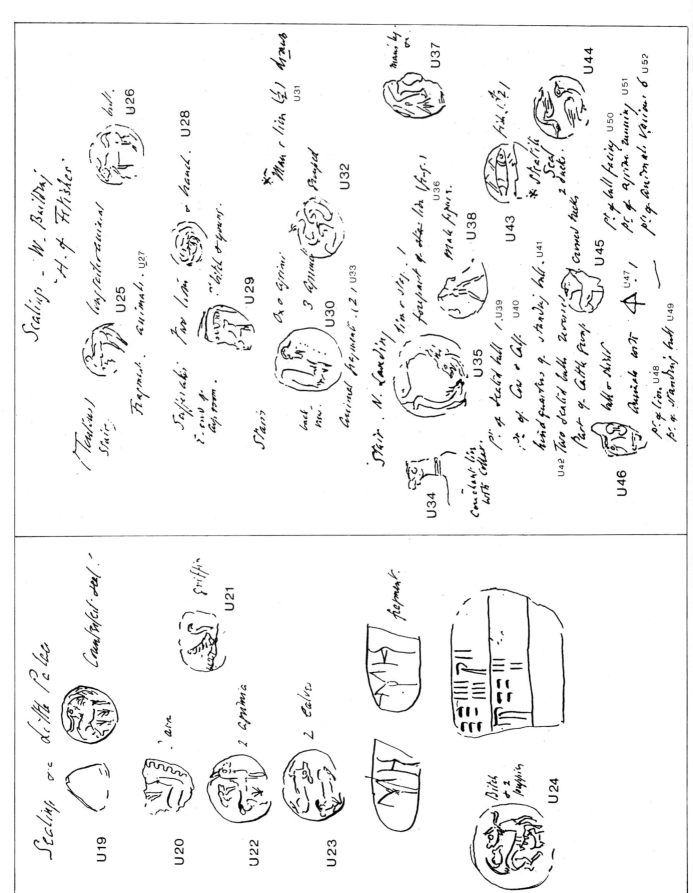

PLATE 47

PLATE 48

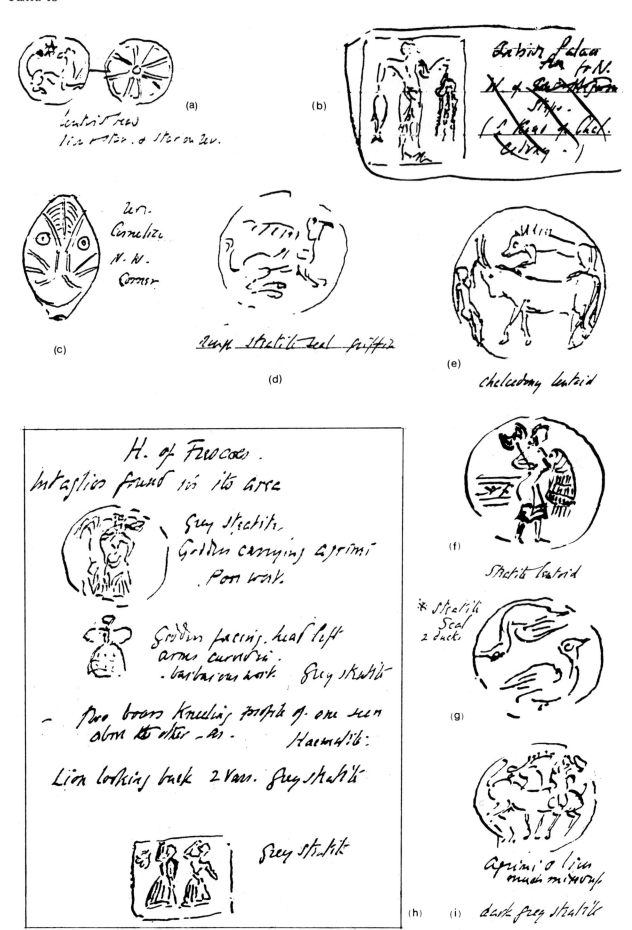

Drawings of seals in Evans's Note-Books. (a) no. 1, (b) no.5, (c) no.4, (d) no.7, (e) no.3, (f) no.8, (g) no. 10, (h) nos.13–18, (i) no.19